Mometrix
TEST PREPARATION

CPA

Financial Accounting & Reporting Exam
Secrets Study Guide

Dear Future Exam Success Story

First of all, **THANK YOU** for purchasing Mometrix study materials!

Second, congratulations! You are one of the few determined test-takers who are committed to doing whatever it takes to excel on your exam. **You have come to the right place.** We developed these study materials with one goal in mind: to deliver you the information you need in a format that's concise and easy to use.

In addition to optimizing your guide for the content of the test, we've outlined our recommended steps for breaking down the preparation process into small, attainable goals so you can make sure you stay on track.

We've also analyzed the entire test-taking process, identifying the most common pitfalls and showing how you can overcome them and be ready for any curveball the test throws you.

Standardized testing is one of the biggest obstacles on your road to success, which only increases the importance of doing well in the high-pressure, high-stakes environment of test day. Your results on this test could have a significant impact on your future, and this guide provides the information and practical advice to help you achieve your full potential on test day.

Your success is our success

We would love to hear from you! If you would like to share the story of your exam success or if you have any questions or comments in regard to our products, please contact us at **800-673-8175** or **support@mometrix.com**.

Thanks again for your business and we wish you continued success!

Sincerely,
The Mometrix Test Preparation Team

Need more help? Check out our flashcards at:
http://MometrixFlashcards.com/CPA

Written and edited by the Mometrix Exam Secrets Test Prep Team
Printed in the United States of America

Table of Contents

Introduction

Thank you for purchasing this resource! You have made the choice to prepare yourself for a test that could have a huge impact on your future, and this guide is designed to help you be fully ready for test day. Obviously, it's important to have a solid understanding of the test material, but you also need to be prepared for the unique environment and stressors of the test, so that you can perform to the best of your abilities.

For this purpose, the first section that appears in this guide is the **Secret Keys**. We've devoted countless hours to meticulously researching what works and what doesn't, and we've boiled down our findings to the five most impactful steps you can take to improve your performance on the test. We start at the beginning with study planning and move through the preparation process, all the way to the testing strategies that will help you get the most out of what you know when you're finally sitting in front of the test.

We recommend that you start preparing for your test as far in advance as possible. However, if you've bought this guide as a last-minute study resource and only have a few days before your test, we recommend that you skip over the first two Secret Keys since they address a long-term study plan.

If you struggle with **test anxiety**, we strongly encourage you to check out our recommendations for how you can overcome it. Test anxiety is a formidable foe, but it can be beaten, and we want to make sure you have the tools you need to defeat it.

Secret Key #1 – Plan Big, Study Small

There's a lot riding on your performance. If you want to ace this test, you're going to need to keep your skills sharp and the material fresh in your mind. You need a plan that lets you review everything you need to know while still fitting in your schedule. We'll break this strategy down into three categories.

Information Organization

Start with the information you already have: the official test outline. From this, you can make a complete list of all the concepts you need to cover before the test. Organize these concepts into groups that can be studied together, and create a list of any related vocabulary you need to learn so you can brush up on any difficult terms. You'll want to keep this vocabulary list handy once you actually start studying since you may need to add to it along the way.

Time Management

Once you have your set of study concepts, decide how to spread them out over the time you have left before the test. Break your study plan into small, clear goals so you have a manageable task for each day and know exactly what you're doing. Then just focus on one small step at a time. When you manage your time this way, you don't need to spend hours at a time studying. Studying a small block of content for a short period each day helps you retain information better and avoid stressing over how much you have left to do. You can relax knowing that you have a plan to cover everything in time. In order for this strategy to be effective though, you have to start studying early and stick to your schedule. Avoid the exhaustion and futility that comes from last-minute cramming!

Study Environment

The environment you study in has a big impact on your learning. Studying in a coffee shop, while probably more enjoyable, is not likely to be as fruitful as studying in a quiet room. It's important to keep distractions to a minimum. You're only planning to study for a short block of time, so make the most of it. Don't pause to check your phone or get up to find a snack. It's also important to **avoid multitasking**. Research has consistently shown that multitasking will make your studying dramatically less effective. Your study area should also be comfortable and well-lit so you don't have the distraction of straining your eyes or sitting on an uncomfortable chair.

The time of day you study is also important. You want to be rested and alert. Don't wait until just before bedtime. Study when you'll be most likely to comprehend and remember. Even better, if you know what time of day your test will be, set that time aside for study. That way your brain will be used to working on that subject at that specific time and you'll have a better chance of recalling information.

Finally, it can be helpful to team up with others who are studying for the same test. Your actual studying should be done in as isolated an environment as possible, but the work of organizing the information and setting up the study plan can be divided up. In between study sessions, you can discuss with your teammates the concepts that you're all studying and quiz each other on the details. Just be sure that your teammates are as serious about the test as you are. If you find that your study time is being replaced with social time, you might need to find a new team.

Secret Key #2 – Make Your Studying Count

You're devoting a lot of time and effort to preparing for this test, so you want to be absolutely certain it will pay off. This means doing more than just reading the content and hoping you can remember it on test day. It's important to make every minute of study count. There are two main areas you can focus on to make your studying count.

Retention

It doesn't matter how much time you study if you can't remember the material. You need to make sure you are retaining the concepts. To check your retention of the information you're learning, try recalling it at later times with minimal prompting. Try carrying around flashcards and glance at one or two from time to time or ask a friend who's also studying for the test to quiz you.

To enhance your retention, look for ways to put the information into practice so that you can apply it rather than simply recalling it. If you're using the information in practical ways, it will be much easier to remember. Similarly, it helps to solidify a concept in your mind if you're not only reading it to yourself but also explaining it to someone else. Ask a friend to let you teach them about a concept you're a little shaky on (or speak aloud to an imaginary audience if necessary). As you try to summarize, define, give examples, and answer your friend's questions, you'll understand the concepts better and they will stay with you longer. Finally, step back for a big picture view and ask yourself how each piece of information fits with the whole subject. When you link the different concepts together and see them working together as a whole, it's easier to remember the individual components.

Finally, practice showing your work on any multi-step problems, even if you're just studying. Writing out each step you take to solve a problem will help solidify the process in your mind, and you'll be more likely to remember it during the test.

Modality

Modality simply refers to the means or method by which you study. Choosing a study modality that fits your own individual learning style is crucial. No two people learn best in exactly the same way, so it's important to know your strengths and use them to your advantage.

For example, if you learn best by visualization, focus on visualizing a concept in your mind and draw an image or a diagram. Try color-coding your notes, illustrating them, or creating symbols that will trigger your mind to recall a learned concept. If you learn best by hearing or discussing information, find a study partner who learns the same way or read aloud to yourself. Think about how to put the information in your own words. Imagine that you are giving a lecture on the topic and record yourself so you can listen to it later.

For any learning style, flashcards can be helpful. Organize the information so you can take advantage of spare moments to review. Underline key words or phrases. Use different colors for different categories. Mnemonic devices (such as creating a short list in which every item starts with the same letter) can also help with retention. Find what works best for you and use it to store the information in your mind most effectively and easily.

Secret Key #3 – Practice the Right Way

Your success on test day depends not only on how many hours you put into preparing, but also on whether you prepared the right way. It's good to check along the way to see if your studying is paying off. One of the most effective ways to do this is by taking practice tests to evaluate your progress. Practice tests are useful because they show exactly where you need to improve. Every time you take a practice test, pay special attention to these three groups of questions:

- The questions you got wrong
- The questions you had to guess on, even if you guessed right
- The questions you found difficult or slow to work through

This will show you exactly what your weak areas are, and where you need to devote more study time. Ask yourself why each of these questions gave you trouble. Was it because you didn't understand the material? Was it because you didn't remember the vocabulary? Do you need more repetitions on this type of question to build speed and confidence? Dig into those questions and figure out how you can strengthen your weak areas as you go back to review the material.

Additionally, many practice tests have a section explaining the answer choices. It can be tempting to read the explanation and think that you now have a good understanding of the concept. However, an explanation likely only covers part of the question's broader context. Even if the explanation makes perfect sense, **go back and investigate** every concept related to the question until you're positive you have a thorough understanding.

As you go along, keep in mind that the practice test is just that: practice. Memorizing these questions and answers will not be very helpful on the actual test because it is unlikely to have any of the same exact questions. If you only know the right answers to the sample questions, you won't be prepared for the real thing. **Study the concepts** until you understand them fully, and then you'll be able to answer any question that shows up on the test.

It's important to wait on the practice tests until you're ready. If you take a test on your first day of study, you may be overwhelmed by the amount of material covered and how much you need to learn. Work up to it gradually.

On test day, you'll need to be prepared for answering questions, managing your time, and using the test-taking strategies you've learned. It's a lot to balance, like a mental marathon that will have a big impact on your future. Like training for a marathon, you'll need to start slowly and work your way up. When test day arrives, you'll be ready.

Start with the strategies you've read in the first two Secret Keys—plan your course and study in the way that works best for you. If you have time, consider using multiple study resources to get different approaches to the same concepts. It can be helpful to see difficult concepts from more than one angle. Then find a good source for practice tests. Many times, the test website will suggest potential study resources or provide sample tests.

Practice Test Strategy

If you're able to find at least three practice tests, we recommend this strategy:

Untimed and Open-Book Practice

Take the first test with no time constraints and with your notes and study guide handy. Take your time and focus on applying the strategies you've learned.

Timed and Open-Book Practice

Take the second practice test open-book as well, but set a timer and practice pacing yourself to finish in time.

Timed and Closed-Book Practice

Take any other practice tests as if it were test day. Set a timer and put away your study materials. Sit at a table or desk in a quiet room, imagine yourself at the testing center, and answer questions as quickly and accurately as possible.

Keep repeating timed and closed-book tests on a regular basis until you run out of practice tests or it's time for the actual test. Your mind will be ready for the schedule and stress of test day, and you'll be able to focus on recalling the material you've learned.

Secret Key #4 – Pace Yourself

Once you're fully prepared for the material on the test, your biggest challenge on test day will be managing your time. Just knowing that the clock is ticking can make you panic even if you have plenty of time left. Work on pacing yourself so you can build confidence against the time constraints of the exam. Pacing is a difficult skill to master, especially in a high-pressure environment, so **practice is vital**.

Set time expectations for your pace based on how much time is available. For example, if a section has 60 questions and the time limit is 30 minutes, you know you have to average 30 seconds or less per question in order to answer them all. Although 30 seconds is the hard limit, set 25 seconds per question as your goal, so you reserve extra time to spend on harder questions. When you budget extra time for the harder questions, you no longer have any reason to stress when those questions take longer to answer.

Don't let this time expectation distract you from working through the test at a calm, steady pace, but keep it in mind so you don't spend too much time on any one question. Recognize that taking extra time on one question you don't understand may keep you from answering two that you do understand later in the test. If your time limit for a question is up and you're still not sure of the answer, mark it and move on, and come back to it later if the time and the test format allow. If the testing format doesn't allow you to return to earlier questions, just make an educated guess; then put it out of your mind and move on.

On the easier questions, be careful not to rush. It may seem wise to hurry through them so you have more time for the challenging ones, but it's not worth missing one if you know the concept and just didn't take the time to read the question fully. Work efficiently but make sure you understand the question and have looked at all of the answer choices, since more than one may seem right at first.

Even if you're paying attention to the time, you may find yourself a little behind at some point. You should speed up to get back on track, but do so wisely. Don't panic; just take a few seconds less on each question until you're caught up. Don't guess without thinking, but do look through the answer choices and eliminate any you know are wrong. If you can get down to two choices, it is often worthwhile to guess from those. Once you've chosen an answer, move on and don't dwell on any that you skipped or had to hurry through. If a question was taking too long, chances are it was one of the harder ones, so you weren't as likely to get it right anyway.

On the other hand, if you find yourself getting ahead of schedule, it may be beneficial to slow down a little. The more quickly you work, the more likely you are to make a careless mistake that will affect your score. You've budgeted time for each question, so don't be afraid to spend that time. Practice an efficient but careful pace to get the most out of the time you have.

Secret Key #5 – Have a Plan for Guessing

When you're taking the test, you may find yourself stuck on a question. Some of the answer choices seem better than others, but you don't see the one answer choice that is obviously correct. What do you do?

The scenario described above is very common, yet most test takers have not effectively prepared for it. Developing and practicing a plan for guessing may be one of the single most effective uses of your time as you get ready for the exam.

In developing your plan for guessing, there are three questions to address:

- When should you start the guessing process?
- How should you narrow down the choices?
- Which answer should you choose?

When to Start the Guessing Process

Unless your plan for guessing is to select C every time (which, despite its merits, is not what we recommend), you need to leave yourself enough time to apply your answer elimination strategies. Since you have a limited amount of time for each question, that means that if you're going to give yourself the best shot at guessing correctly, you have to decide quickly whether or not you will guess.

Of course, the best-case scenario is that you don't have to guess at all, so first, see if you can answer the question based on your knowledge of the subject and basic reasoning skills. Focus on the key words in the question and try to jog your memory of related topics. Give yourself a chance to bring the knowledge to mind, but once you realize that you don't have (or you can't access) the knowledge you need to answer the question, it's time to start the guessing process.

It's almost always better to start the guessing process too early than too late. It only takes a few seconds to remember something and answer the question from knowledge. Carefully eliminating wrong answer choices takes longer. Plus, going through the process of eliminating answer choices can actually help jog your memory.

Summary: Start the guessing process as soon as you decide that you can't answer the question based on your knowledge.

How to Narrow Down the Choices

The next chapter in this book (**Test-Taking Strategies**) includes a wide range of strategies for how to approach questions and how to look for answer choices to eliminate. You will definitely want to read those carefully, practice them, and figure out which ones work best for you. Here though, we're going to address a mindset rather than a particular strategy.

Your odds of guessing an answer correctly depend on how many options you are choosing from.

Number of options left	5	4	3	2	1
Odds of guessing correctly	20%	25%	33%	50%	100%

You can see from this chart just how valuable it is to be able to eliminate incorrect answers and make an educated guess, but there are two things that many test takers do that cause them to miss out on the benefits of guessing:

- Accidentally eliminating the correct answer
- Selecting an answer based on an impression

We'll look at the first one here, and the second one in the next section.

To avoid accidentally eliminating the correct answer, we recommend a thought exercise called **the $5 challenge**. In this challenge, you only eliminate an answer choice from contention if you are willing to bet $5 on it being wrong. Why $5? Five dollars is a small but not insignificant amount of money. It's an amount you could afford to lose but wouldn't want to throw away. And while losing $5 once might not hurt too much, doing it twenty times will set you back $100. In the same way, each small decision you make—eliminating a choice here, guessing on a question there—won't by itself impact your score very much, but when you put them all together, they can make a big difference. By holding each answer choice elimination decision to a higher standard, you can reduce the risk of accidentally eliminating the correct answer.

The $5 challenge can also be applied in a positive sense: If you are willing to bet $5 that an answer choice *is* correct, go ahead and mark it as correct.

Summary: Only eliminate an answer choice if you are willing to bet $5 that it is wrong.

Which Answer to Choose

You're taking the test. You've run into a hard question and decided you'll have to guess. You've eliminated all the answer choices you're willing to bet $5 on. Now you have to pick an answer. Why do we even need to talk about this? Why can't you just pick whichever one you feel like when the time comes?

The answer to these questions is that if you don't come into the test with a plan, you'll rely on your impression to select an answer choice, and if you do that, you risk falling into a trap. The test writers know that everyone who takes their test will be guessing on some of the questions, so they intentionally write wrong answer choices to seem plausible. You still have to pick an answer though, and if the wrong answer choices are designed to look right, how can you ever be sure that you're not falling for their trap? The best solution we've found to this dilemma is to take the decision out of your hands entirely. Here is the process we recommend:

Once you've eliminated any choices that you are confident (willing to bet $5) are wrong, select the first remaining choice as your answer.

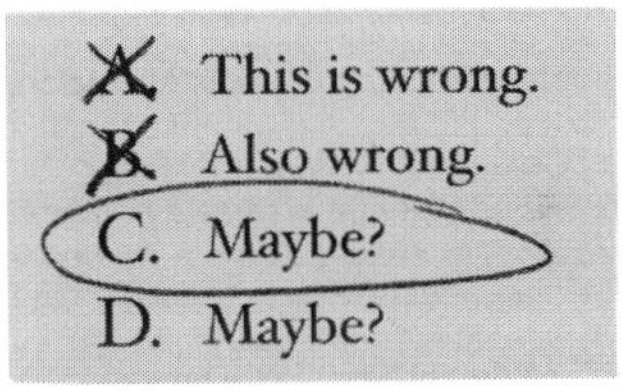

Whether you choose to select the first remaining choice, the second, or the last, the important thing is that you use some preselected standard. Using this approach guarantees that you will not be enticed into selecting an answer choice that looks right, because you are not basing your decision on how the answer choices look.

This is not meant to make you question your knowledge. Instead, it is to help you recognize the difference between your knowledge and your impressions. There's a huge difference between thinking an answer is right because of what you know, and thinking an answer is right because it looks or sounds like it should be right.

Summary: To ensure that your selection is appropriately random, make a predetermined selection from among all answer choices you have not eliminated.

Test-Taking Strategies

This section contains a list of test-taking strategies that you may find helpful as you work through the test. By taking what you know and applying logical thought, you can maximize your chances of answering any question correctly!

It is very important to realize that every question is different and every person is different: no single strategy will work on every question, and no single strategy will work for every person. That's why we've included all of them here, so you can try them out and determine which ones work best for different types of questions and which ones work best for you.

Question Strategies

✓ Read Carefully

Read the question and the answer choices carefully. Don't miss the question because you misread the terms. You have plenty of time to read each question thoroughly and make sure you understand what is being asked. Yet a happy medium must be attained, so don't waste too much time. You must read carefully and efficiently.

✓ Contextual Clues

Look for contextual clues. If the question includes a word you are not familiar with, look at the immediate context for some indication of what the word might mean. Contextual clues can often give you all the information you need to decipher the meaning of an unfamiliar word. Even if you can't determine the meaning, you may be able to narrow down the possibilities enough to make a solid guess at the answer to the question.

✓ Prefixes

If you're having trouble with a word in the question or answer choices, try dissecting it. Take advantage of every clue that the word might include. Prefixes can be a huge help. Usually, they allow you to determine a basic meaning. *Pre-* means before, *post-* means after, *pro-* is positive, *de-* is negative. From prefixes, you can get an idea of the general meaning of the word and try to put it into context.

✓ Hedge Words

Watch out for critical hedge words, such as *likely, may, can, often, almost, mostly, usually, generally, rarely,* and *sometimes*. Question writers insert these hedge phrases to cover every possibility. Often an answer choice will be wrong simply because it leaves no room for exception. Be on guard for answer choices that have definitive words such as *exactly* and *always*.

✓ Switchback Words

Stay alert for *switchbacks*. These are the words and phrases frequently used to alert you to shifts in thought. The most common switchback words are *but, although,* and *however*. Others include *nevertheless, on the other hand, even though, while, in spite of, despite,* and *regardless of*. Switchback words are important to catch because they can change the direction of the question or an answer choice.

⊘ Face Value

When in doubt, use common sense. Accept the situation in the problem at face value. Don't read too much into it. These problems will not require you to make wild assumptions. If you have to go beyond creativity and warp time or space in order to have an answer choice fit the question, then you should move on and consider the other answer choices. These are normal problems rooted in reality. The applicable relationship or explanation may not be readily apparent, but it is there for you to figure out. Use your common sense to interpret anything that isn't clear.

Answer Choice Strategies

⊘ Answer Selection

The most thorough way to pick an answer choice is to identify and eliminate wrong answers until only one is left, then confirm it is the correct answer. Sometimes an answer choice may immediately seem right, but be careful. The test writers will usually put more than one reasonable answer choice on each question, so take a second to read all of them and make sure that the other choices are not equally obvious. As long as you have time left, it is better to read every answer choice than to pick the first one that looks right without checking the others.

⊘ Answer Choice Families

An answer choice family consists of two (in rare cases, three) answer choices that are very similar in construction and cannot all be true at the same time. If you see two answer choices that are direct opposites or parallels, one of them is usually the correct answer. For instance, if one answer choice says that quantity *x* increases and another either says that quantity *x* decreases (opposite) or says that quantity *y* increases (parallel), then those answer choices would fall into the same family. An answer choice that doesn't match the construction of the answer choice family is more likely to be incorrect. Most questions will not have answer choice families, but when they do appear, you should be prepared to recognize them.

⊘ Eliminate Answers

Eliminate answer choices as soon as you realize they are wrong, but make sure you consider all possibilities. If you are eliminating answer choices and realize that the last one you are left with is also wrong, don't panic. Start over and consider each choice again. There may be something you missed the first time that you will realize on the second pass.

⊘ Avoid Fact Traps

Don't be distracted by an answer choice that is factually true but doesn't answer the question. You are looking for the choice that answers the question. Stay focused on what the question is asking for so you don't accidentally pick an answer that is true but incorrect. Always go back to the question and make sure the answer choice you've selected actually answers the question and is not merely a true statement.

⊘ Extreme Statements

In general, you should avoid answers that put forth extreme actions as standard practice or proclaim controversial ideas as established fact. An answer choice that states the "process should be used in certain situations, if..." is much more likely to be correct than one that states the "process should be discontinued completely." The first is a calm rational statement and doesn't even make a definitive, uncompromising stance, using a hedge word *if* to provide wiggle room, whereas the second choice is far more extreme.

⊘ Benchmark

As you read through the answer choices and you come across one that seems to answer the question well, mentally select that answer choice. This is not your final answer, but it's the one that will help you evaluate the other answer choices. The one that you selected is your benchmark or standard for judging each of the other answer choices. Every other answer choice must be compared to your benchmark. That choice is correct until proven otherwise by another answer choice beating it. If you find a better answer, then that one becomes your new benchmark. Once you've decided that no other choice answers the question as well as your benchmark, you have your final answer.

⊘ Predict the Answer

Before you even start looking at the answer choices, it is often best to try to predict the answer. When you come up with the answer on your own, it is easier to avoid distractions and traps because you will know exactly what to look for. The right answer choice is unlikely to be word-for-word what you came up with, but it should be a close match. Even if you are confident that you have the right answer, you should still take the time to read each option before moving on.

General Strategies

⊘ Tough Questions

If you are stumped on a problem or it appears too hard or too difficult, don't waste time. Move on! Remember though, if you can quickly check for obviously incorrect answer choices, your chances of guessing correctly are greatly improved. Before you completely give up, at least try to knock out a couple of possible answers. Eliminate what you can and then guess at the remaining answer choices before moving on.

⊘ Check Your Work

Since you will probably not know every term listed and the answer to every question, it is important that you get credit for the ones that you do know. Don't miss any questions through careless mistakes. If at all possible, try to take a second to look back over your answer selection and make sure you've selected the correct answer choice and haven't made a costly careless mistake (such as marking an answer choice that you didn't mean to mark). This quick double check should more than pay for itself in caught mistakes for the time it costs.

⊘ Pace Yourself

It's easy to be overwhelmed when you're looking at a page full of questions; your mind is confused and full of random thoughts, and the clock is ticking down faster than you would like. Calm down and maintain the pace that you have set for yourself. Especially as you get down to the last few minutes of the test, don't let the small numbers on the clock make you panic. As long as you are on track by monitoring your pace, you are guaranteed to have time for each question.

⊘ Don't Rush

It is very easy to make errors when you are in a hurry. Maintaining a fast pace in answering questions is pointless if it makes you miss questions that you would have gotten right otherwise. Test writers like to include distracting information and wrong answers that seem right. Taking a little extra time to avoid careless mistakes can make all the difference in your test score. Find a pace that allows you to be confident in the answers that you select.

⊘ KEEP MOVING

Panicking will not help you pass the test, so do your best to stay calm and keep moving. Taking deep breaths and going through the answer elimination steps you practiced can help to break through a stress barrier and keep your pace.

Final Notes

The combination of a solid foundation of content knowledge and the confidence that comes from practicing your plan for applying that knowledge is the key to maximizing your performance on test day. As your foundation of content knowledge is built up and strengthened, you'll find that the strategies included in this chapter become more and more effective in helping you quickly sift through the distractions and traps of the test to isolate the correct answer.

Now that you're preparing to move forward into the test content chapters of this book, be sure to keep your goal in mind. As you read, think about how you will be able to apply this information on the test. If you've already seen sample questions for the test and you have an idea of the question format and style, try to come up with questions of your own that you can answer based on what you're reading. This will give you valuable practice applying your knowledge in the same ways you can expect to on test day.

Good luck and good studying!

Standard Setting

SEC

The SEC is a federal agency whose role is to guard investors from uninformed or misinformed decisions by providing regulation over the exchange of securities. It serves to enforce a series of legislative acts, including the law which brought the SEC into existence, the Securities Exchange Act of 1934. One of the SEC's main requirements of companies for the accurate disclosure of their operations is to file an annual report, Form 10-K, and Form 10-Q. Formed in 1934, the SEC arose during the Great Depression in response to the stock market crash of 1929, with the purpose of regulating the stock market and inhibiting corporate fraud. In regulating the securities market, the SEC is currently responsible for legislating and explicating seven major laws: the Securities Act of 1933, the Securities Exchange Act of 1934, the Trust Indenture Act of 1939, the Investment Company Act of 1940, the Investment Advisers Act of 1940, the Sarbanes-Oxley Act of 2002, and the Credit Rating Agency Reform Act of 2006.

Influence on Accounting Principles

The SEC possesses the authority to modify, abolish, or create any regulations it deems necessary in order to execute the intent of the law, which requires companies to helpfully and transparently disclose information to investors and others who have interest in the companies. The SEC has very broad and far-ranging powers in this regard. Towards this end, the SEC also interacts with the Financial Accounting Standards Board (FASB), which is central to setting accounting standards for the private sector. This includes working with the Emerging Issues Task Force (EITF) of the FASB, whose purpose is to pinpoint relevant accounting issues for the FASB. The Chief Accountant of the SEC attends EITF meetings to maintain awareness and dialogue on these issues. Whenever the SEC wishes to provide advice or instruction to the FASB, such information is contained in either a Financial Reporting Release (FRR) or a Staff Accounting Bulletin (SAB) which defines the problem and (perhaps) steps towards a solution until the FASB creates new rules in response.

IASB

The International Accounting Standards Board (IASB) was founded on April 1, 2001 to serve as an independent standard-setting committee for the IFRS Foundation. The IASB works toward the global convergence of accounting standards by cultivating and implementing International Financial Reporting Standards (IFRS). They also desire to assess the needs for financial reporting which arise from developing economies and small and medium-sized entities (SMEs). The board was originally created with fifteen members, but the trustees of the IASB voted in January 2009 to expand the number of members in the IASB to sixteen by July 2012. According to the IFRS website (www.ifrs.org), the terms of the board members begin and end at various dates and persist for various durations, but through the site one can easily learn who the current board members are. The board members display a range of national diversity, ranging from America to the UK, the Netherlands, Sweden, Germany, France, Brazil, South Africa, India, South Korea, Japan, and China.

GASB

Despite its name, the Governmental Accounting Standards Board (GASB) is not a governmental body, but is rather a private-sector board, formed in 1984 as a section of the Financial Accounting Foundation (FAF), whose objective is to form and enhance accounting standards for state and local governments in the US Due to the differences between for-profit accounting and governmental accounting, it is important that a separate standard-setting body be erected to clarify the relevant issues and provide clear standards. The GASB's declarations are recognized as the authoritative standards of generally accepted accounting principles (GAAP) for state and local governmental accounting.

Conceptual Framework

Sub-Models of the Accounting Model

The three main sub-models are financial position, results of operations, and the statement of cash flows. The financial position sub-model is summarized by the equation Assets = Liabilities + Equity. It specifies all of a company's resources (assets), stating which of the resources are owned by others (liabilities) and which by the company owners (equity)., and is communicated through a balance sheet. The results of operation sub-model is summarized by the equation Revenues – Expenses = Net Income. It states how successful the company is in making a profit with its main operations, and is communicated through an income statement. The statement of cash flows sub-model is summarized by the equation Operating Cash +/– Investing Cash +/– Financing Cash = Change in Cash. It seeks to communicate how the company has handled all of its cash inflows and outflows over a given period.

Assumptions on Which Accounting Theory Is Based

The four underlying assumptions upon which financial accounting theory is based are:

- Economic Entity – The business is separate and distinct from the owners. Business finances are not co-mingled with owner finances.
- Going Concern – There is no reason or belief that the business is going to liquidate in the near future. If the business is expected to be liquidated, then net realizable values are utilized as opposed to historical costs.
- Unit-of-Measure – The unit of measure for accounting is monetary. Costs incurred in the business over time must presume that the purchasing power of the dollar remains constant, even though it does not allow inclusion of the variable inflation. To be more accurate in the dollar's value, businesses can utilize SFAS 89, Financial Reporting and Changing Prices to update the purchasing power of the dollar.
- Periodicity – Information is prepared and reported at periodic intervals (monthly, quarterly, and annually). To make the information that is produced by financial accounting more pertinent in decision making, it must be timely.

Accounting Principles

The following are eight accounting principles:

- Materiality – Included information must be sufficiently large to be relevant. Whether an error is considered large enough to affect the judgment of someone relying on the information depends on:
    - Relative importance of the data
    - Cost-benefit relationship of the additional accuracy
    - Possible confusion when too many details are considered
- Consistency – The information becomes more useful if it is presented in the same manner time after time. Consistency makes comparison and trend analysis easier, and provides an additional measure against management manipulation of the financial figures.
- Full Disclosure – To enhance decision making by all parties, all pertinent accounting information should be complete and understandable.
- Conservatism – The usual approach, if the appropriate accounting application is not certain or if there is conflicting data, is to understate income or net assets. This would not apply if the difference amount is material.

- Historical Cost – Any assets or liabilities that are acquired by a business are recorded at the time of purchase by the cost or cash equivalent amount defined by an "arm's-length transaction" or a transaction that is between unrelated parties.
- Revenue Recognition – Income is reported when earned, regardless of when the payment is received. This is usually denoted when the two following conditions are satisfied:
    - Earnings process is or nearly is complete.
    - Revenues are recognized at time of exchange, e.g., sale, percentage of completion, production, installments, or cost recovery basis.
- Matching – All expenses incurred when revenues were being generated must be reported at the same time to match revenues to related expenses.
- Objectivity – Estimates and measurements must be fair, reasonable, based on fact, and unbiased.

Financial and Physical Capital Maintenance Concepts

The concept of capital maintenance is critical in distinguishing return on investment from return of investment. Both investors and businesses invest financial resources with the expectation that the investment will generate more financial resources than were invested. A return on financial capital results only if the amount of net assets at the end of a period exceeds the net assets at the beginning of the period after excluding the effects of transactions with owners. In contrast, under the physical capital maintenance concept, a return on physical capital results only if the physical productive capacity at the end of the period exceeds the physical productive capacity at the beginning of the period, after excluding the effects of transactions with owners. The principal difference between the two capital maintenance concepts involves the effects of price changes during a period on assets while held and liabilities while owed. Under the financial capital concept, if the effects of price changes are recognized, they are holding gains and losses and are included in the return on capital. Under the physical capital concept, those changes would be recognized but would be capital maintenance adjustments that would be included directly in equity and not included in return on capital.

Financial Reporting

Goals

The following are five goals of financial reporting:

- To provide information in monetary values for transactions in a specific time period.
- To meet the needs of the people receiving the reports, including external readers, in determining financial performance.
- To enable those who make the financial decisions, such as investors and creditors, to make capable judgments regarding the business.
- To report how the business generates earnings and cash flows and represent how the business uses economic resources, secures additional funds, and distributes dividends.
- To indicate how management performs in guiding the business.

Business Entities

The knowledge of a business's operations is crucial for those making decisions regarding the business, such as investors. Therefore, financial reporting has the objective of accurately and comprehensively communicating this information to others, and the primary purpose is to make such information helpful for those who are making decisions based off of this financial data. This data-communication is largely accomplished through financial statements such as the balance sheet and income statement.

Not-for-Profit (Nongovernmental) Entities

Financial reporting for nonprofit entities differs in the purpose for which the financial statements are given. Many nonprofit entities reveal their financial information not necessarily to assist users in making informed financial decisions, but to communicate how wisely or responsibly the funds are, in fact, being used. Otherwise, the FASB has determined that nonprofit financial reporting should be identical, or at least very similar, to financial reporting with for-profit entities.

State and Local Governmental Entities

The Governmental Accounting Standards Board (GASB) is the primary rule-creating body for state and local governmental entities, laying down generally accepted accounting principles for them. Governmental entities lack the profit motive present in commercial entities, since they are constituted by legislative authorities in the service of the populace and merely accept taxes as their source of revenue. Governmental bodies are also given a number of legal restrictions to regulate their use of budgetary funds.

Financial Reporting and Presentation

BALANCE SHEET

A balance sheet is a monetary representation, meeting the standards of generally accepted accounting principles, of assets, liabilities, and owner's equity at a certain point in time. The accounting format and the reporting format are the two most commonly used configurations. In the accounting format, there are two columns. One side lists the assets of the entity while the other column contains the liabilities and the owner's equity. In the reporting format, a single column is used to document assets, liabilities, and owner's equity, in that order.

ASSET SECTION

One portion of the balance sheet is dedicated to assets. The assets include potential economic benefits and are listed in order of liquidity, usually in the categories of current and noncurrent assets:

- Current assets –Can easily be converted into cash or will be used within a normal business cycle or one year. These include cash, cash equivalents, accounts receivable, and inventory.
- Noncurrent assets – Will be used after or beyond a normal business cycle or one year. These include property, plant, and equipment; intangible assets (such as goodwill or intellectual property); and investments.

LIABILITY SECTION

Liabilities are the debts and obligations of a business, and are listed on the balance sheet by due date and current or long-term status.

- Current Liabilities – Debts that must be paid in the short-term, generally within a year. Usually presented in order of payment due date or priority of payment.
- Long-Term Liabilities – Business debts that are due over the longer term, which is generally considered longer than one year.
- Valuation Accounts – Similar to valuation accounts for assets, these are associated with the original liability, i.e., not separate assets or liabilities. The changes, such as discounts on bonds, affect the amount of the liability.

OWNER'S EQUITY SECTION

Owner's equity is defined by SFAC 6 as the remaining interest in assets after liabilities have been deducted. Originally created by the investments of the owners, it can increase by the addition of investors and decrease when it is distributed amongst its investors. It can also fluctuate because of business operations. When there is a sole owner, owner's equity is called proprietor's equity. In a partnership, equity accounts are set up for each partner, allowing for individualized accounting of investments, income, or withdrawals.

When a corporation is formed, accounts are determined by their source. Minimum contributed capital is determined by incorporation regulations or state law. Retained earnings are a result of accumulated earnings minus losses and dividends and are considered a resource to use when growing the business.

INCOME STATEMENT

A company's income statement reports its revenues and expenses for a given period of time, showing how the revenues result in a given net income. The expenses listed on the income statement include all the charges against the revenues, such as write-offs and taxes. Income statements also should include disclosures for extraordinary and unusual items. Taken as a whole, then, the income statement indicates the success or failure of a company's profitable activities. This provides users of the financial statements with information to appraise a company's past performance and predict its future effectiveness

Single-Step and Multi-Step Formats

The single-step and multi-step formats for an income statement differ most clearly in the fact that the multi-step gives information for more types of intermediate incomes, listing gross income, operating income, pretax income, and after-tax income. By contrast, the single-step format generally lists only pretax income and net income, excluding gross income and operating income. In addition, the formats differ according to their classification for statement items; multi-step formats emphasize a more functional or object categorization for various statement items.

Statement of Retained Earnings

A statement of retained earnings gives a final summation on the changes in retained earnings over a given period. Included in the statement are profits (or losses) from the company's main operations, dividends paid out, the issuance or redemption of stock, and any other changes to retained earnings. Since the retained earnings is a sort of final destination for profit and loss accounts, the statement of retained earnings helps to supplement the income statement by noting how the revenues and expenses reported on the income statement translate into final effects upon retained earnings.

Comprehensive Income

Comprehensive income measures the difference in equity across a time period, except for any changes in equity arising from owner investments and distributions. Consequently, comprehensive income is comprised of net income and other comprehensive income (OCI). Net income involves the company's essential or primary revenue-seeking activities, whereas other comprehensive income can include such things as gains and losses on securities and gains and losses from foreign-currency transactions.

The three acceptable ways of reporting comprehensive income are:

- Statement of income and comprehensive income
- Statement of income and separate statement of comprehensive income
- Statement of changes in equity

As comprehensive income is composed of two elements, net income and other comprehensive income (OCI), it is very important that the business classify the comprehensive income elements by their origin. This can include pension liability adjustments, foreign currency holdings, unrealized gains or losses pertaining to certain investments, or certain gains or losses on hedging activities. It is prudent that the business list the accumulated balance of OCI separate from retained earnings and additions to capital in the equity section of the statement of financial position. It is also required that the balances for each classification remain separate, whether in the statement of financial position, in the statement of changes in equity, or as an addendum to the financial statements.

Statement of Changes in Equity

A statement of changes in equity describes all the transitions in a company's equity accounts, including how the company's equity is and was constituted. The statement should report the company's total comprehensive income, and it should provide a reconciliation between the carrying amounts for each component of equity at the beginning and end of the period being reported. Components of equity include share capital and share premiums, retained earnings, unrealized gains on investments or foreign-currency transactions, and other things.

Statement of Cash Flows

A statement of cash flows is responsible for communicating to readers the amount and uses of cash funds for a business over a time period. It is divided into three sections: operating, investing, and financing. The operating section involves all those cash flows tied up with the company's main operations, that is, the same activities which are used to determine net income. The investing section tracks the cash movement for transactions involving securities (available-for-sale and held-to-maturity) and property, plant, and equipment, in addition to collections and sales on purchased loans. The financing section includes cash from the repayment of debts, the payment of dividends, the issuance of stock, and any other finance activities (such as derivatives).

Direct Method vs. Indirect Method

The direct method for reporting the statement of cash flows simply categorizes all cash flows into the three subsections (operating, investing, and financing), lists the total cash in- and outflows for each of those, and then states the cumulative change in cash for the time period. The indirect method, on the other hand, also incorporates information from the income statement directly into the statement of cash flows. Usually this means that net income will be a starting point in the statement, which is then adjusted to account for non-cash line items and thus reconcile the net income to the net cash provided by operating activities. When these adjustments are made to net income, it is important to remember that assets decrease the adjusted amount while liabilities increase it.

Operating, Investing, and Financing Activities

Operating activities could properly be called the most significant and central of a company's activities, as they involve the production and delivery of the company's featured goods and services. Examples of cash flows from operating activities (according to IAS 7) would be receipts from the sale of goods or services, interest received on loans, payments to suppliers, payments to employees, and purchases of merchandise. Investing activities involve investment in financial markets or subsidiary companies, in addition to the purchase of capital assets. Examples of investing activities would be the purchase of land or a building, loans made to suppliers or received from customers, and payments related to mergers and acquisitions. Financing activities include those activities whereby the company either receives investments or pays out dividends. Also included are any activities which are significant to long-term debt and equity. Examples of financing activities would be payments of dividends, repurchases of company stock, and the repayment of loan principal, including capital leases.

SFAC 7

Statement of Financial Accounting Concepts (SFAC) 7, titled "Using Cash Flow Information and Present Value in Accounting Measurements," is a measurement tool. It provides general rules for the use of present value, especially when the amount of future cash flows, their timing, or both are uncertain. The measurements apply only to those figures based on future cash flows such as initial recognition, fresh-start measurement, or specific amortization. The FASB describes fresh-start measurements as measurements not related to past figures or means of obtaining those figures. Present values in this instance are only used as a basis for fair market value for fresh-start measurements and initial recognition.

Role of Notes to Financial Statements

Since the goal of financial accounting and reporting is to accurately reflect a company's activities to those dependent upon knowledge of the company, and since some of the company's activities will inevitably be miscellaneous or difficult to categorize, the notes to the financial statement serve as a catch-all for such information. Placing such information in the notes is also helpful to keep the main financial statements from being cluttered with information that needs to be reported but ought to be kept in a less prominent place. The notes will include such information as accounting methodology, stock option compensation details, contingent liabilities, reasons for impairments, and other things.

Consolidated Financial Statements

Consolidated financial statements exist when one company owns over 50% of the voting shares of a different firm. The consolidated financial statements provide a cumulative look at the parent company and the subsidiary (or subsidiaries). This is due to the "single entity" accounting principle, to show the performance of a group of companies as if they were a single unit. The material difference between consolidated and non-consolidated financial statements is in the transactions between parents and subsidiaries; the consolidated financial statements would keep those from being double-counted.

Big GAAP and Little GAAP

Because compliance with GAAP can be so burdensome for smaller companies, the FASB has made efforts to allow alternative and simpler accounting criteria for non-public companies. Overseeing this is the *Private Company Council* (PCC), established by the FASB.

"Big GAAP" refers to the ordinary GAAP framework as assumed by public entities, whereas "little GAAP" refers to the simpler framework as assumed by non-public/private entities.

As of 2014, the PCC has issued three pronouncements providing "alternative accounting approaches" for particular accounting issues: goodwill, derivatives (specifically, interest rate swaps), and variable interest entities (VIEs) involved in leases.

SEC Reporting Requirements

Form 10-K

The Form 10-K is an annual report which public companies must file with the SEC. It is very comprehensive about the company's performance—more comprehensive than the firm's annual report—including such information as company history, organizational structure, subsidiaries, executive compensation, and audited financial statements. It must be made available to any shareholder who requests it. In addition, public companies must file the form with the SEC within 60 days after year-end if they are "large accelerated filers" (having an annual cash flow above $700 million), within 75 days after year-end if they are "accelerated filers" (having an annual cash flow above $75 million), or within 90 days after year-end if they are "nonaccelerated filers." The Form 10-K is divided into four parts and fifteen schedules. Part I contains information on the business, properties, legal proceedings, and matters to be voted upon by security holders. Part II includes selected financial data, management's discussion and analysis, and expressions of disagreement with accountants on financial reporting. Part III presents information on directors and executive officers, including their compensation. Part IV contains exhibits and financial statement schedules. (This is not an exhaustive list on Form 10-K content, however.)

Form 10-Q

The Form 10-Q is an annual report which public companies must file with the SEC on a quarterly basis—except for the fourth quarter, when the company files a Form 10-K. The Form 10-Q is similar to the annual report in terms of the content and amount of information presented, disclosing the company's financial position up to that point in time. Unlike the Form 10-K, the Form 10-Q discloses unaudited financial statements. Both "large accelerated filers" and "accelerated filers" must file the Form 10-Q within 40 days after quarter-end, whereas "nonaccelerated filers" may file it within 45 days after quarter-end.

Other Financial Statement Presentations

SPFs

In the United States, GAAP is the ordinary standard for accounting systems. Therefore, a special purpose framework (SPF) is an accounting basis which is not in conformity with GAAP. This does not mean that SPFs are in violation of any accounting laws; rather, SPFs are used when GAAP is not required. Specifically, SPFs can be helpful when GAAP is unnecessary due to loan covenants, regulatory requirements, or other circumstances. Previously, SPFs were referred to as Other Comprehensive Bases of Accounting (OCBOAs).

Cash Basis of Accounting

In cash-basis accounting, events and transactions are reported or recognized only when cash is itself disbursed or received. This stands opposed to accrual-basis accounting, when events and transactions are recognized only when revenues are earned or expenses are incurred. Accrual-basis accounting involves when a company gains the right to receive or obligation to pay in transaction, whereas cash-basis accounting involves only those actual points in time when the cash is itself transferred.

Modified Cash Basis of Accounting

The modified cash basis of accounting is a hybrid of the cash basis and accrual basis of accounting. A great example of a problem with a pure cash basis of accounting is long-term construction. If a construction company constructs a building over a long period of time, then it might be that there are many expenses to be paid out during that time period and a huge inflow of cash at the end. In this case, a cash basis of accounting would present misleading financial statements during that time period; the income would be too low and then too high. A modified cash basis seeks to solve this by recognizing accruals for long-term balance sheet items and cash receipts or payments for short-term balance sheet items, even though it does not fully commit to a pure accrual system for all revenues and expenses.

Income Tax Basis of Accounting

The income tax basis of accounting essentially tries to reproduce a financial statement as it would look if the company were calculating its income tax return. Events are recognized and accounted for when either taxable income or deductible expenses are recognized on the tax return. A primary motivation for companies to use an income tax basis of accounting is to avoid producing different sets of financial statements with different bases for accounting (e.g., income tax basis and GAAP). Instead, whatever the company utilizes for its tax return, it presents to others as being done upon the income tax basis of accounting.

Changing Cash-Based Financial Information to Accrual-Based Financial Statements

Companies may need to change cash-based accounting systems to accrual-based for financial reporting purposes. The company uses cash entries to record payments received and expenses paid. This holds true for all items, except fixed assets, that are capitalized and depreciated. In the accounting ledger, there will be two entries: one called "current for the cash-based system" and one called "correct for the accrual-based system." A balance sheet will show two parts that relate to changes from current to correct. For example, accounts receivable changes will be reflected in the sales account, accounts payable changes will show up in purchases or expenditures, and items that might have been prepaid will now show as an expense. There are multiple equations for changing from current to correct-based reporting, but it is not necessary to remember them, as they can be figured out from T-style recording accounting.

Personal Finance Statement and Treatment of Assets and Liabilities

A personal financial statement for an individual, husband and wife, or a family are all comprised of the same two financial statements.

- Statement of Financial Condition – States estimated current values of assets, estimated current liabilities, estimated income taxes, and a net worth correlating to a particular date.
- Statement of Changes in Net Worth – Gives details on the gains or losses in net worth over a specific time period.

Assets are recorded at their estimated current value less material disposal costs, because it is the fair value that would be expected to be exchanged between two knowledgeable parties. Liabilities are recorded as either the discounted amount of cash to be paid or the current cash settlement amount, whichever is smaller.

Income Tax Payable and Estimated Income Tax in Personal Financial Statements

Personal financial statements include information about income tax payable and estimated income tax. Income tax payable includes unpaid income taxes as of the date of the financial statement. Estimated income tax is calculated on the differences between the estimated current values of assets and the estimated current amounts of liabilities and their tax bases, including consideration of negative tax bases of tax shelters. The calculation must include applicable tax laws, recapture provisions, and carryovers. The statements should indicate that the income tax provision will probably differ from the amount of taxes that might eventually be paid, as well as describe methods and assumptions used to compute estimated income taxes, unused loss carryforwards and any other unused deductions and credits with their expiration periods.

Financial Statements of Employee Benefit Plans or Trusts

The financial statements for employee benefit plans or trusts to a great degree reflect the financial statements for ordinary companies. Their role is to accurately reflect how the funds of the benefit plan or trust are being utilized or invested. The specific financial statements involved in accounting for an employee benefit plan or trust are (1) a statement of net assets available for benefits, (2) a statement of changes in net assets available for benefits, (3) a statement of a benefit plan's obligations, (4) a statement of changes in a benefit plan's obligations, and (5) notes to the financial statements.

Liquidation Basis Financial Statements

Entities whose liquidation is "imminent" must issue liquidation basis financial statements. Liquidation counts as imminent if either of the following conditions obtains:

- those with the due authority have approved a liquidation plan, and the chance of that plan's being thwarted, or of the entity's returning from liquidation, is remote
- the entity is required to undergo liquidation (usually bankruptcy).

The fundamental accounting difference involved in a liquidation basis is that the entity must provide a *statement of net assets in liquidation*, along with a *statement of changes in net assets in liquidation*. This requires valuing assets according to what the entity expects to receive upon sale. The entity also must accrue costs it expects to incur in the assets' sale. Liabilities generally remain the same, though they are not restated even if the entity expects to be legally relieved of them. Of course, the statements must include disclosures describing the liquidation plan and the methods in preparing the liquidation basis statements. Two types of companies are exempt from the requirement to follow liquidation-basis accounting: investment companies registered per the Investment Company Act of 1940 (for they are legally unable to differently measure their assets), and limited-life entities which have already specified a liquidation plan in their governing documents from their inception.

Financial Statement Accounts

Cash and Cash Equivalents

An asset's liquidity is its ability to be easily converted into cash. Therefore, cash is necessarily the most liquid asset (often making it the first item in the current assets section), and cash equivalents are those assets which are easily convertible into cash. Cash can consist of currency on hand and petty cash funds, while cash equivalents can consist of negotiable paper (such as checks and money orders), money market funds, marketable securities, commercial paper, and other things.

Bank Reconciliation

Bank reconciliations are performed at timely intervals to locate and correct errors and to provide a check point of figures. There can be activity in the ledgers which does not show up on the bank statement, such as outstanding checks, deposits or withdrawals not yet shown on the statement, or petty cash located on the premises. Another reason differences occur is due to amounts on the bank statements that need to be recorded in the ledgers. Examples are interest earned, bank service charges, returned checks, and payments made by the bank. Human error on both the business and bank side is a reason to reconcile the ledger and bank statement.

Cash Discounts

Cash discounts are typically deemed an expense if they are recognized when the cash payment is made within the discount time frame. This is ordinary if it recurs on a regular basis. If the discount on the receivables is irregular, an account to document these changes must be created or the sales can be shown without the discounts. The net amount is used because the values for the sales are cash and receivables are more accurate than fair market values. In both net and gross methods, sales and accounts receivable are documented without the discount for more accurate values. But if the sales account is used with the gross entry method, the discount is shown directly under the sales entry and subtracted accordingly. If the net method is used, discounts expected for year-end receivables are documented, but usually these late adjustments are not shown because they remain constant.

Receivables

Receivables are assets of a business founded upon the obligations of others to provide payment to the business. The most common type of receivable are accounts receivable, which arise out of customer obligations to pay the business for an ordinary sale. Another type of receivable are notes receivable, which consist of formal promissory notes signed by another party (whether a customer or not) unconditionally to repay the company. They might arise from overdue accounts receivable or loans to others, and they can be either interest-bearing or non-interest-bearing. These two are the primary types of receivables, but others exist as well, such as interest receivable: the total of interest accrued for the company but not yet paid to it.

Efficiency Ratios

Operational efficiency shows that a business is able to make income and use assets effectively. Below are two ratios that demonstrate operational efficiency:

- Receivables turnover is a function of net credit sales divided by average net receivables. The ratio shows how efficient credit and collection policies are. It is also an indicator of the quality of receivables. The average net receivables can be found by adding the beginning and ending net receivables and dividing by two. This figure should also include any trade notes receivable.
- Days sales outstanding (DSO) is an estimate of how many days are required to collect receivables. The ratio formula is (Total Receivables/Total Credit Sales) x Number of Days. A business has the choice of using 360, 300, or 250 as the average number of business days in a year.

Recording Bad Debts

Two methods for recording bad debts are as follows:

- Direct write-off method – The bad debt is expensed or written off in the same time period that it occurs. It is only allowable under generally accepted accounting principles when the amount is inconsequential. The direct write-off method is appropriate for tax accounting purposes.
- Allowance method – This method uses an estimate of bad debts and makes a correlating account for those debts, called "bad debt expense" and "allowance for bad debts." When the amount is written off, the figures are offset by recordings in allowance for bad debts and accounts receivable. The annual charge to bad debt expense is ascertained by either annual sales or year-end accounts receivable. If income statement accounting is more prominent, then annual sales percentage amounts are utilized, owing to the fact that the bad debts correlate to sales. Balance sheet accounting coordinates year-end accounts receivable percentages with bad debt. The percentage of bad debt can be obtained from total accounts receivable or separate accounts. Specific amounts which are written off offset each other in accounts receivable and allowance accounts, so that the net receivables remains unchanged.

Criteria for Control of Accounts Receivable to Be Transferred

Three criteria must be met before control of accounts receivable are lost by the transferor. They are as follows:

- The assets transferred can no longer be influenced by the transferor, or any businesses that are associated with the transferor.
- The assets transferred can be pledged or exchanged without any arbitrary determent by the transferee. This also holds true for special-purpose business investors.
- The transferor has been ineffective in his control of the assets and that control has been handed over in a contract that specifies the repurchase or payment before the maturity date at a pre-specified price or all the assets must be returned.

PLEDGING AND FACTORING ACCOUNTS RECEIVABLE

When a business can't wait for accounts receivables collections for cash, it can decide to pledge or factor accounts receivable:

- Pledging – Uses accounts receivable as collateral for loans. This does not affect how the receivables are collected. The pledged accounts are reviewed by the lender to determine validity and then used as security. The borrower is obligated to pay back the loan regardless of whether or not the receivables are indeed received. It is important for financial recording purposes that the accounts receivable are marked as pledged and the debt denoted as secured by the receivables.
- Factoring – Occurs when receivables are sold to a financing company or factor. In order for the transaction to occur, the customer obligated to pay the receivables must be properly informed, so that future payments are made to the factor. The factor is entitled to rewards and risk involved in collecting receivables. The factor assumes the risk at a cost to the business receiving the cash early. The factor can receive interest for the time between obtaining the receivables and time when receivables are due and can charge the business a percentage of estimated uncollectible receivables.

INVENTORY

The term inventory means physical items that are in the business's possession for sale or to be used to produce items for sale. The inventory's value is determined by the cost of each item and the number of items. The cost can represent the cash or cash equivalent paid for the items or the fair market value of the items. Also included in the value of the inventory is the amount paid to receive the inventory items and prepare the items for sale, handling fees, and spoilage. If it is manufacturing inventory, then the costs must also incorporate direct materials, direct labor, and factory overhead, both direct and indirect. An important criterion for the items to be accounted for as inventory is that the business has ownership.

TYPES OF ACCOUNTING FOR PHYSICAL INVENTORY

The two types of accounting for physical inventory are the Periodic Inventory System and the Perpetual Inventory System:

- The Periodic Inventory System counts and prices each individual item when it is inventoried on a regular basis. Cost of goods sold is the amount that remains when the beginning inventory combined with net purchases is reduced by the ending inventory. During this time period, there are no entries made to the inventory account, thus the name "periodic."
- The Perpetual Inventory System maintains a constant total of units on hand, coming into, and delivered out of inventory as they occur. The financial records reflect the inflow and outflow in the inventory account.

VALUING INVENTORY

The following are four methods of valuing inventory:

- LIFO – The *last* inventory items purchased are treated as the first ones removed, in which case the remaining inventory will be valued at the price of inventory purchased *earlier*. For instance, if 600 objects were purchased on Jan. 1 at $10 apiece and 400 more on Feb. 1 at $12 apiece, and if there were 750 objects remaining on Feb. 15, then the inventory value would be (600 * $10) + (150 * $12) = $7,800.

- FIFO – The *first* inventory items purchased are treated as the first ones removed, in which case the remaining inventory will be valued at the price of inventory purchased *later*. For instance, given the above example, the inventory value on Feb. 15 would be (400 * $12) + (350 * $10) = $8,300.
- Weighted average – The inventory items are all treated as of equal cost, depending on the quantity and price of inventory items historically purchased. For instance, in the above example, suppose that the purchase of 400 objects on Feb. 1 resulted in a total inventory of 1,000. The total cost of the inventory to that point would be (600 * $10) + (400 * $12) = $10,800, in which case the entire inventory would be revalued at ($10,800 / 1,000) = $10.80/unit. Thus, if 750 units remained on Feb. 15, they would be valued at (750 * $10.80) = $8,100.
- Moving average – This is similar to the weighted average method of valuing inventory, except that it specifically revalues the unit cost of inventory after each purchase.

Inventory Ratios

Two common ratios that pertain to inventory are inventory turnover and days sales in inventory. Inventory turnover is a ratio of cost of goods sold divided by the average inventory (beginning inventory plus ending inventory divided by two). If the number is low, it represents slow-moving items, which is a bad sign for business. If the inventory is perishable, such as food, then the inventory turnover ratio should be high. The inventory turnover ratio is an indicator of how hard the inventory is working for the business. Days sales in inventory (DSI) is calculated by dividing the number of days in a year, 365, by the inventory turnover rate. This number is an indicator of the management of the items in inventory. If the items are being held or stored for too long before being sold, it could mean that better use of company funds is possible.

Situations in Which Business Has Ownership of Inventory but Not Physical Possession

Four situations in which a business has ownership of inventory, but does not physically hold the items are:

- Goods in Transit from Vendor –If the items are shipped Free On Board (F.O.B.) shipping point, the business receiving the items counts them as inventory when the items are shipped.
- Goods in Transit to Customer – When the items are shipped F.O.B. destination point to the customer, the business must continue to show the items in inventory until the customer receives them.
- Goods on Consignment – If an item is out on consignment or in the care of someone else, the item must still be shown on the business's inventory as it is considered a temporary condition. However, if the item is sold while on consignment, the inventory accounting should reflect that change in ownership.
- Transportation Charges – Will be included as part of cost of ownership of the inventory if the F.O.B. is destination point.

Property, Plant, and Equipment

Property, plant, and equipment are tangible assets which a business attains to use for its normal operations long-term. Various accounting issues tied up with property, plant, and equipment include acquisition (which can involve deferred payment plans, group purchases, nonmonetary transactions, self-construction, etc.), cost recovery (which can involve depreciation and depletion), impairment (with respect to assets held for use, held for disposal by sale, and held for disposal other than sale), and disposal (whether voluntary or involuntary).

Property, plant, and equipment acquisition costs can include the following:

- Purchase for cash – The amount paid in cash or its equivalent minus any business or quantity reductions in the price.
- Purchase on deferred payment plan – If a cash equivalent amount cannot be determined for the fixed asset, the present value of the asset should be computed from forecasted payments with another asset's interest rate.
- Purchase by issuance of securities – The value of the asset can be determined in the following ways:
    - Either the fair market value of the asset or securities issued, whichever is easily recognizable.
    - If the securities are being actively traded, the security value should be used.
    - If bonds are being used and there is not a convenient market value, the present value of the asset and its principal payments less an implied interest rate would be used.
    - If the securities do not have a fair market value, the appraised value of the asset can be used.
- Self-construction – When an asset is constructed to be used by the business, the costs pertaining to the asset should include costs of material, labor, and overhead.
- Interest costs – These pertain to interest that is capitalized over the construction period of the asset. It is part of the cost of obtaining the asset and is written off over its useful life. 1. To qualify for interest capitalization, it must be a constructed asset, an asset that is constructed for the business's repeatable use, assets obtained for the business's use that dictate down payments or a series of payments, or construction projects that become for sale or lease, such as ships or real estate property. 2. The amount of interest that would have been avoided if the asset had not been obtained is the amount of interest to be capitalized. If there is a specific rate applied to the asset, then it should be used unless it causes the average accumulated expenditures to exceed the amount borrowed with the specific rate. The excess would then be capitalized at a weighted average of the rates that pertain to borrowed amounts by the business. 3. The interest amount should be applied to the average amount of collected costs of the asset during the period. 4. The interest capitalized in a time period cannot be more than total interest costs for that same time period. 5. Interest capitalized costs cannot be determined by interest costs offset by interest earned by the business.
- Nonreciprocal transfers – When nonmonetary assets are reassigned to a stockholder or another business, the gain or loss of the fair, appraised, or net book value at the time of transfer must be documented.
- Exceptions – Occur in the following instances:
    - Business combinations – use SFAS 141.
    - If nonmonetary assets are transferred between businesses under the same management or main company.
    - Transfers between corporate joint businesses and the owners of the joint businesses.
    - Receipt of nonmonetary assets or services by the reporting business issuing stock.
    - Stock received with respect to stock dividends or stock splits.
    - When a business receives equity in another business as a result of the transfer of assets.

Methods for Accounting for Long Term Construction Contracts

The two generally accepted methods used in accounting for long-term construction contracts are completed-contract and the percentage-of-completion. The completed-contract method accounts for revenue and profit when the agreed-upon factors in the contract are completed. In this method, income is recognized only when the contract is completed, or substantially so. All costs and related revenues are reported as deferred items in the balance sheet until that time. The percentage-of-completion method depends on good estimates of contract revenues, costs, and time to completion that are responsible and trustworthy enough for accounting purposes. Usually companies that employ this method utilize contracts as a major portion of revenue operations. The major advantage to this method is the ability to receive and show income, while the major disadvantage is being able to produce reliable estimates.

Capitalizing Interest Associated with Acquiring Assets

According to SFAS 34, it is necessary to capitalize interest associated with assets that must be prepared over a period of time for use by the business. It doesn't matter if the item is being manufactured for sale by the business or is being built for the business's use. If a company acquires a building, then it does not qualify, but if it builds the building or hires another firm to build the building, it does. Also, land being held by the business, but not utilized, cannot have its interest capitalized. The interest figure is calculated by multiplying the average accumulated expenses during construction by the interest rate and by the construction period. It is looked upon as an amount that could be avoided if the project were not undertaken. The time period starts when investment is made in the asset, work begins on the asset, and interest costs have begun. It ends with completion or near completion of the project. Only inactivity on the project will cause the interest capitalization to be upheld. Capitalizing interest enables the business to account for obtaining the asset and to correlate the cost of the asset with revenue over the same time period.

Straight-Line Depreciation and Accelerated Depreciation

Depreciation is an accounting function which decreases the book value of an asset over a specific time period, i.e., its useful life. Depreciation can either decrease the value of the asset itself or distribute the cost of an asset over the period during which it is used.

- Straight-line depreciation – Determined by taking the historical cost less the salvage value, divided by the asset's useful life. This is a set figure used for each accounting period.
- Accelerated depreciation – Takes into account that an asset may be more useful or productive early in its life and an asset may become obsolete prior to the end of its useful life, and consequently depreciates the assets more in its earlier years.

Fractional-Year Depreciation and Depletion

As an asset may be obtained at any time during a financial record period, it is important to be able to account for segments of time of depreciation or fractional-year depreciation. There are three methods for this type of depreciation:

- At the time of purchase, the asset is depreciated for that year and is not depreciated in the year it is disposed of.
- A year's worth of depreciation can be halved and included in the year the asset is obtained with the second half expensed the year the asset is disposed of.
- A more detailed or accurate method is to determine a year's depreciation expense and then divide it by months, weeks, days, or hours and use that figure according to how long the asset was utilized.

Depletion costs are associated with natural resources, which do not have a fixed service life. The cost of the natural resource is a function of four sources. They are acquisition of asset, exploration costs, development costs and restoration costs. The total cost is divided by the estimated total resource to give a depletion charge per unit of resource.

Multiple-Asset Depreciation and Variable Charge Methods

Multiple-asset depreciation is used when items can be categorized together to limit the amount of calculations required. Group depreciation and composite depreciation are two methods used:

- Group depreciation – Puts similar types of assets, including length of service life, together so that one depreciation amount can be assessed and used for all.
- Composite depreciation – Puts similar types of assets, but with varying lengths of service, together. Initially a composite depreciation is formulated from the sum of straight-line depreciation for each asset. That sum is divided by the total original cost to determine the composite depreciation rate. The composite depreciation rate is multiplied by the total original cost to arrive at the annual composite depreciation figure for the group of assets.

Variable charge method is related to production or usage as opposed to time and is therefore a variable cost. The depreciation expense can be expressed in units, hours, or whatever is appropriate. This amount is found by subtracting the salvage value from the original cost of the asset and dividing by the total life or usage in units, hours, etc.

Voluntary and Involuntary Fixed Asset Disposal

Voluntary fixed asset disposal must credit the asset account for the cost, less the accumulated depreciation, debiting the correct account for funds received and acknowledging a gain or loss to balance the accounts. If the disposal involves an exchange of nonmonetary assets, regulations regarding the exchange of assets must be used. If a fire, flood, storm, or other act of nature causes destruction of property, buildings, or equipment, this is considered involuntary fixed asset disposal. The remaining value of the assets is shown as a loss for that specific time period. If insurance covers the casualty losses, the business may have a gain or a loss depending upon the coverage. If the involuntary nonmonetary loss results in a gain or loss, it needs to be documented, even if settlements received are used to purchase replacement nonmonetary assets. The conversion expense should also include cleanup cost and removal and disposal of lost assets. Costs pertaining to acquiring new nonmonetary assets are included with the new assets.

Uses and Costs Associated with Investments in Securities

A business will invest funds in short-term securities when it has extra amounts of cash not required for day-to-day operations. Additional funds could also be funneled into long-term securities. These monies are then able to produce more money. Equity securities that are held for potential earnings, appreciation, or investor control are additional uses for the extra funds. When an investment is considered temporary, it has both marketability and intent. The intent of the holders is to obtain cash or other current assets. Long-term investments are all other forms of security investments that are not considered marketable or having intent. When a security is purchased, the recorded amount includes cost, broker's fees, taxes, and all other fees pertaining to obtaining the security.

Financial Assets at Fair Value Through Profit or Loss

According to IAS 39, all financial assets must be categorized into one of four categories, depending upon the purpose for which the asset is bought and held. One of these categories is financial assets at fair value through profit or loss, which is itself composed of two sub-categories, "financial assets held specifically for trading purposes" and "financial assets to be measured at fair value under the fair value option designation." When initially acquired, they are recognized at fair value, and they are generally classified as current assets.

AFS SECURITIES

An available-for-sale (AFS) security is a debt or equity security which is purchased with the intent that it will be sold before it reaches maturity or (for securities without a maturity date) before a sufficiently long period of time. AFS securities are reported at fair value, and any changes in value for the security while it is held across accounting periods are included in other comprehensive income (OCI).

HTM SECURITIES

A held-to-maturity (HTM) security is a debt security which a business intends (and is able) to hold to maturity. These securities are not recognized at fair value when reported, but are instead recognized at their amortized cost, leaving the reported value unaffected by changes in financial markets. They can receive no adjustments, then, for holding gains or losses.

JV INVESTMENTS

A joint venture (JV) investment is an agreement between two or more businesses whereby the parties decide to invest equity in a new entity with new assets to achieve some purpose. The businesses which are parties to the joint venture, since they share equity ownership, consequently share in the expenses and revenues of the new entity. Sometimes joint ventures are done internationally in order to expand a company's market.

EQUITY METHOD OF ACCOUNTING FOR INVESTMENTS

When a business is accounting for its investment in another business, the equity method is employed when the amount invested equals 20-50% of the outstanding common stock. In such a case, the investor has a meaningful influence over the business, so the equity method is appropriate. The equity method has the cash dividends reducing the carrying amount of investment, and the income is the *pro rata* share of the business's earnings. There are two types of cases when it is necessary to make changes in the equity accounting method:

- Changes from Equity Method – If stock ownership falls below 20%, it is required that the accounting method be changed to the cost method. The value on the date when the change takes place becomes the cost basis for the new accounting method. If the entire ownership is liquidated, then the gain or loss should be reflected by the difference between the carrying price and the sold price.
- Changes to Equity Method – This occurs when the investor increases ownership in the business to greater than 20%. Just as adjustments are made when a business purchases a subsidiary, these changes need now to be reflected in the new accounting method, such as investment account, results of operations, and retained earnings. Changes should correlate with the percentage of ownership or stock.

INVESTMENT PROPERTY

Investment property is any property held by an entity for the purpose of gaining rental revenue, capital appreciation, or both. Examples of investment property include land held for undetermined future use, vacant buildings planned to be leased out to others, and property that is being developed for future purposes as an investment property. Property held for use or held for sale as part of the ordinary activities of the business does not qualify as investment property.

SECURITIZATION

Securitization is the process of pooling and repackaging cash-flow producing financial assets, or a group of assets, such as mortgage-backed securities, and transforming them into securities that are sold to investors. Often there are markets for these assets, and the benefit is lower financing costs in borrowing when using these assets as collateral. Liquidity and lower credit risk are additional benefits. The security mechanism is developed by a transferor, also known as an issuer or sponsor. The mechanism could also be a qualifying special-purpose entity, used to purchase assets and issue securities. The process could involve a transfer made to a trust with the trust issuing the securities. It is known as one-tier or two-tier depending on which method is used. The benefits to the security mechanism occur in interest in assets and sold cash flows. The type of assets, income tax assessments, and returns determine how securities are selected.

Intangible Assets

Intangible assets are non-monetary assets which are not physical and therefore cannot be sensed or physically measured. Intangible assets can be legal (intellectual property) or competitive (e.g., executive or employee knowledge). Competitive intangible assets are significant in how much they affect the business's success—the main source of competitive advantage—while not being "ownable" as an asset. Legal intangible assets can also be classified as either definite or indefinite, depending on the expected life or functionality of the asset.

The following are three types of intangible assets:

- Patent – A particular type of right for a product or process that is valuable to the possessor of the right. If the right is obtained through external means, then the costs can be capitalized. Additional costs that can be capitalized are costs necessary to protect the patent. However, if a legal ruling is determined against the patent, those costs associated with defending the patent are shown as expenses at that time. Costs associated with internal evolvement of the patent are shown as incurred expenses.
- Franchise – A right which is given to run a business under the name and regulations of that business in a specific location. All important costs associated with obtaining the franchise should be capitalized, including future cash payments represented by calculating the present value with an applicable interest rate. Continuing service fees that are based on a percentage of revenues become part of the current operating expenses.
- License – A permission from the government to operate the business. If the amount to obtain the license is large, it should be capitalized and amortized over either its service life or its legal life, whichever is shorter.

Differences in Accounting for Externally and Internally Acquired Intangible Assets

Intangible assets that are acquired externally, or outside the business, are recorded at fair market value. An exception is assets which were procured in a bundle of assets within the transfer. The value of the assets are recorded according to their individual fair market value only, and do not include any goodwill. If an intangible asset is developed internally, then all the costs associated with the development, maintenance, or restoration of the asset, including goodwill, are recorded as expenses when they occur, if they cannot be easily recognized and do not seem to have a limited life.

Finite Useful Life, Amortization Period, and Amortization Method

The finite useful life of an intangible asset is a determined amount of time that the asset will be contributing either directly or indirectly to future cash flows. The period of time should include expected use time of the asset or legal, regulatory, or contractual considerations that would put a limit on the usefulness of the asset. Extending those agreements and their costs is also a consideration. The time factor should also include whether the asset may become obsolete, the threat of competition, other outside business influences, and whether the asset has maintenance issues. The amortization period is the gradual and periodic reduction of the cost of the intangible asset over its useful life.

Amortization method – If the usefulness of the asset can easily be determined, then the reduction should reflect that amount, whether it is greater in the beginning of its availability and being used or whether it is at the end and may be possibly extended. If the determination cannot be made, then straight-line amortization is the best method.

Residual Value and Reevaluation

Residual value – The dollar amount a company expects to receive when it disposes of an asset or the value at the end of the asset's useful life to the company. The residual value of an intangible asset is assumed to be zero unless at the end of its useful life the asset is expected to have a useful life to another entity and (a) the reporting entity has a commitment from a third party to purchase the asset at the end of its useful life or (b) the residual value can be determined by reference to an exchange transaction in an existing market for that asset and that market is expected to exist at the end of the asset's useful life.

Reevaluation – The usefulness of the asset should be reassessed at each accounting period to ensure that the amortization should continue or whether changes need to be made to reflect any differences in the situation.

- If the amortized life should be lengthened or shortened, depending upon the circumstances, then a new amortized amount should correspond to the change.
- If the asset is determined to have an indefinite life, then the amortized amount is no longer valid and is not necessary, and the asset must be assessed yearly for impairment.

Goodwill

Goodwill is the sum total of the value of a business which exceeds its assets. Since a company can have intelligent and efficient workers, a good reputation, top-notch leadership, and other valuable competitive intangible assets, the value of an entity taken as a whole will often exceed the value of its stated assets—and that difference is goodwill.

While goodwill is an intangible asset, it is often reported as a line item separate from intangible assets on the balance sheet. Goodwill is tested for impairment on an annual basis (at least) with a two-step process. First, one must seek to identify potential impairment by comparing the fair value of a reporting unit (i.e. a discrete profit-generating center of an entity, or a component of one) to its carrying amount. If the fair value is greater than the carrying amount, then goodwill is not impaired. However, if goodwill is impaired, then the second step is to measure the extent of impairment as the difference between the fair value and the carrying amount.

Accrued Liabilities and Kinds of Payables

Accrued liabilities are liabilities which have been incurred but not yet paid or categorized as accounts payable. They are liabilities incurred but which have not yet generated an official account or invoice. An example of an accrued liability would be accrued wages payable. Among the different types of payables are accounts payable, notes payable, and dividends payable. Accounts payable are liabilities incurred within a business's ordinary activities in the transactions of various products. Notes payable are loans from banks or other lending institutions, and they can be either short-term or long-term, as well as interest-bearing or non-interest-bearing. Dividends payable are liabilities incurred to shareholders for cash dividends.

CONTINGENT LIABILITIES

Contingent liabilities occur when outcomes of situations won't be known until after the balance sheet is reported. The difference between a contingency and a liability is that a liability is a known factor but the amount may be unclear. In a contingency, whether or not there is actually a liability is the unknown. A contingent liability may become an actual liability if one or more events occur or fail to occur. The estimation of the amount of the contingent liability, as well as the accounting treatment and disclosure requirements, depend on the likelihood of actual loss. Examples of contingent liabilities are product warranty commitments, product defect responsibilities, requirements pertaining to coupons or premiums, and outstanding insurance claims or lawsuits.

CLASSIFICATIONS

Classifications depend upon the probability that happenings in the future will cause the contingent loss to occur and that the amount can be reasonably estimated:

- Probable – The contingency loss is most likely to occur. If the loss can be reasonably estimated, it is recorded by debiting an expense account and crediting a liability account. If the amount of the contingent loss can't be reasonably estimated, the contingency should be disclosed in financial statement footnotes only.
- Reasonably possible – Somewhere between probable and remote. If the loss is reasonably possible, no charge is made to income and the details of the contingency must be disclosed in the notes to the financial statements.
- Remote – If the loss seems very unlikely to occur, it is considered remote. Typically with remote possibility, disclosure is not necessary. However, disclosures should be made when there is a guarantee of indebtedness of others, banks' standby letters of credit, or guarantees to repurchase receivables.

ROLE OF DEFERRED REVENUES

Whereas accrued liabilities are incurred but not yet paid, deferred revenues are revenues received but not yet earned. Since deferred revenues represent an obligation of the company to provide a good or service without receiving additional payment in return, they constitute a liability on the company's balance sheet. (They may also be accounted for as "unearned revenues.") Examples of deferred revenues are rent paid in advance to a landlord and gift cards purchased at a store. In both cases, the business ought to have a journal entry for the initial cash inflow (debiting cash and crediting deferred or unearned revenues) and a later journal entry for the earning of the revenues (debiting deferred/unearned revenues and crediting revenue).

LONG-TERM DEBT

Long-term debt consists of all formal obligations to pay a customer, lending institution, or someone else, which the company does not expect to extinguish with its current assets (i.e., paid back within one year) or through the formation of current liabilities. Long-term notes payable are a clear example of long-term debt, and another example would be the result of financially restructuring short-term debt into a longer repayment period.

LONG-TERM LIABILITIES

Long-term liabilities encompass all commitments that will not require the liquidation of current assets or the generation of current liabilities. This includes long-term notes payable, short-term commitments that are refinanced, and bonds payable. Per SFAS 47, the total amounts of maturities and sinking fund conditions of long-term commitments must be reported for each of the five years following the dates of the latest balance sheet period.

Discount or premium amortization applies when the discount or premium is amortized over the lifetime of the commitment to produce a fixed rate of interest that is implemented to the carrying amount of the commitment at the beginning of a reporting period. According to APB 21, any amortization method can be used if the determined amount of interest is not significantly different than the amount found using the effective interest method.

NOTES PAYABLE

Notes payable are any formal financial instruments in which one party promises unconditionally to pay an amount of money to another party and (sometimes) according to a particular pay schedule. They differ from accounts payable in that they involve a written promissory note, while the usual paperwork for an account payable is nothing more than an invoice for an ordinary business transaction (e.g. purchasing supplies). Notes payable can be categorized as notes issued for cash and notes exchanged for property, goods, or services.

PREMIUM AND DISCOUNT ON A BOND

A premium occurs when a bond's stated interest rate is higher than the current market interest rate for corresponding financial instruments. In this situation, investors are willing to pay more than face value for the bond. If the stated interest rate is lower than the current market interest rate, the bond will generally be sold at a discount. Discounts and premiums are not reported as separate items by the investor, but are included in the "Investment in Bonds" account. If the bond is a long-term investment, the premiums or discounts have to be amortized from purchase date to maturity date. To determine which interest technique should be utilized to amortize the differences, see Accounting Principles Board (APB) 21. If the differences are immaterial, straight-line amortization can be used.

CONVERTIBLE DEBT

Convertible debt is a form of debt in which the loan's outstanding balance eventually converts in some amount to equity (such as shares in a corporation). Generally, convertible debt financing exists when an investor makes a loan to a startup company with the intent of later transforming that loan into a true investment. An advantage of convertible debt, and the main reason it is utilized, is to stave off negotiations of stock valuation until a later date; for a period of time the "investment" is simply a loan, and so the specific value of the investment can be negotiated in the future.

DEBT EXTINGUISHMENT, IN-SUBSTANCE DEFEASANCE, AND ADVANCE REFUNDING

Debt extinguishment is simply the elimination of a financial obligation and its consequent removal from the company's financial statements (specifically, the balance sheet). Debt is ordinarily extinguished through payment, but can also be extinguished through release, in which the creditor (or the legal system) relieves the debtor of his obligations. The most common example of debt extinguishment through release is bankruptcy. In-substance defeasance is the process by which a debt is removed from the financial statements without yet being canceled. The typical condition in which this occurs is when a company sets aside assets, usually a portfolio of treasury securities, with the intent to use it for the debt's repayment. In-substance defeasance should be accounted for not as a debt extinguishment, but as a separate asset and liability. Advance refunding is the obtaining of new debt in order to repay principal and interest on old, outstanding debt. This is done for the purpose of acquiring lower interest rates, extending the repayment date of the lent money, or eliminating or modifying certain restrictions that might have existed with the older loan.

TROUBLED DEBT RESTRUCTURING AND DEBT RESTRUCTURING

Troubled debt restructuring takes place when a creditor, for either economic or legal grounds correlated to the debtor's financial difficulties, allows the debtor a concession. One concession could be the transfer of assets or an equity interest in the debtor that meets the obligations of the debt. Another concession could be a change in the terms of the contract where the interest rate may be reduced, the maturity date lengthened, or the amount of the original debt and accrued interest reduced. Debt restructuring occurs if the debtor is having difficulty but is able to assume credit at a rate similar to the current rate for nontroubled debt from a different creditor. The difference is that in troubled debt restructuring, the debtor must receive a concession from the creditor. The creditor grants this allowance to protect as much of the investment as possible.

Troubled Debt Restructuring for Debtors and Creditors

Debtors acknowledge and report the difference or gain between the carrying amount of the debt with accrued interest and the total of the future payments stated in the new terms. If assets are transferred after the restructuring, the debtor must acknowledge the difference between the fair value and the carrying amount of the assets transferred as a gain or loss. Creditors acknowledge and report the difference or loss between the fair value of the assets or equity interest received and the reported amount of the receivable plus accrued interest. In accounting principles, the loss is deemed as ordinary. Whatever is received at the time of restructuring, either assets or equity securities, will be recorded at fair value.

Types of Troubled Debt Restructuring

Types of troubled debt restructuring include:

- Transfer of assets from the debtor to the creditor to fully or partially pay back the debt. This includes foreclosure or repossession.
- Receipt by the creditor of equity interest in the debtor, assuming no existing terms for converting debt to equity.
- Modification of debt terms, such as a reduction in the stated interest rate, an extension of the maturity date at an interest rate lower than the current market rate, a reduction in the face or maturity amount, a reduction of accrued interest, or some combination of these.

Debt Covenant Compliance

When a lender makes a loan to a borrower, there may be specific contractual restrictions on what the borrower must do in addition to repaying the sum of the loan. For instance, the borrower might be obligated not to take on more debt, or some companies might be required to comply with specific accounting practices. In total, this obedience to the debt contract constitutes debt covenant compliance. The lender may take certain actions to ensure borrower compliance, such as mandatory audits. And if a borrower is non-compliant, the lender might either permit a grace period to allow the borrower to become compliant or demand immediate repayment of the loan.

Owner's Equity

Owner's equity is the owner's interest in the business. It is what is left of the assets when the liabilities are taken out, per SFAC 6. The form of the owner's equity depends upon the type of ownership interest.

- Owner's equity or net worth is the same as sole proprietorship equity when there is a single equity account.
- If there is a partnership, then there is a capital account for each partner. Their accounts reflect their investments and proportion of income and withdrawals.
- When it is a business organization that has an equity account, it typically has three parts.
  - Capital from contributions, capital stock, and paid-in capital.
  - Retained earnings.

- Composite balance per SFAS 130 that is from other comprehensive income (OCI). OCI has four categories:
  - Foreign currency
  - Pension liability adjustments
  - Unrealized gains and losses on specific investments for debt and equity securities
  - Specific hedging ventures' gains and losses

CAPITAL STOCK

There are three types of capital stock with respect to owner's equity.

- Par value – This is the value stated on the stock itself. If the business were to be liquidated, it is the most the creditors could expect to get back. If a stock is issued and subscribed, then the par value is its legal or stated capital.
- No-par value – If a stock is issued without a stated value, then it is a no-par value stock. This allows the issuer of the stock to avert liability consequences when a stock is issued below a stated or par value or at a discount. The legal or stated capital of the business is represented by the stated or assigned payback of all the no-par value stocks.
- No-par with stated value – Although the stock does not have a stated or par value documented, it is still treated the same as a par value stock.

COMMON STOCK AND PREFERRED STOCK

From an owner's equity point of view:

- Common Stock – Gives one part of the remaining ownership in a corporation. When a person holds the common stock, they are the last to be addressed if the corporation liquidates, and because of this they have higher risk. A common stockholder also has the highest potential compensation. The basic powers that a common stockholder has are the right to vote, dividends, the predominant privilege of purchasing additional stock the corporation may offer, and a share in the distribution of assets should the corporation be dissolved.
- Preferred Stock – Comes with more privileges than common stock. The most notable is that if the corporation should liquidate, the preferred stockholder would have higher ranking in the distribution of assets. Another benefit to being a preferred stockholder is a higher position in the distribution of dividends, prior to the distribution of dividends to the common share stockholder. The dividends are a stated percentage of par or if the stocks are no-par, then a certain dollar amount. Preferred stockholders do not have the privilege of voting.

PREFERRED STOCK

Some attributes of preferred stock are:

- Cumulative – Dividends accrue even if not actually paid, and must be paid before common stock dividends.
- Convertible – Gives the stockholder the choice of exchanging preferred stock for common stock of the same company.
- Callable or redeemable – Preferred stock generally has an unlimited life, but may have a callable feature that gives the issuing corporation the choice of buying back the preferred stock, generally after a stated date.
- Participating or non-participating – Some preferred stocks pay "bonus" dividends based on corporate profits.

Effects of Stock Transactions on Retained Earnings

The effects of certain stock events can either be positive or negative to the retained earnings. The gains or losses in the operations of a corporation can cause either increases or decreases to retained earnings. All dividends cause decreases to retained earnings. Stock splits whose par is reduced proportionately do not cause any effect to retained earnings, but a stock split without proportionate par reduction causes decreases. If the corporation acquires treasury stock using the cost method, then it does not affect retained earnings. However, if the corporation chooses to use the par value method, then there may be no change or a decrease in retained earnings. When a corporation chooses to sell treasury stock using the cost method, it may cause no change or a decrease in retained earnings. The par value method does not affect retained earnings. If the corporation has to make prior period adjustments or specific special changes in accounting principle, then the retained earnings will be adjusted accordingly.

Dividend

When a stockholder is given an appropriate allocation of retained earnings based upon the number and type of stocks owned, that amount is a dividend. If a corporation is being dissolved, then the amount or share of the business the stockholder receives is a liquidating dividend. With the exception of stock dividends, most dividends, whether a rationing of assets or additional liability, cause a reduction in stockholder's equity. When the board of directors officially announces dividends, that date becomes the date of declaration. On the date of declaration, the dividends become a liability with the exception of stock dividends. On the date of record, all the stockholders at that time will receive dividends. If the number of shares outstanding is not the same as the date of declaration, then a journal entry is necessary. The date of payment represents the day the assets are administered.

Bond

A bond is a type of long-term promissory note that can be recorded in the owner's name or can be granted as bearer instruments. While agreeing to pay the principal amount in the future, periodic interest payments over a specific time frame and at a specific interest rate must be made by the borrower.

Serial and Term Bonds, Debenture Bonds, Callable Bonds, and Convertible Bonds

- Serial and term bonds –
  - When a bond requires repayment of the principal in a series of payments, it is deemed a serial bond.
  - When a bond matures on a specific date, it is a term bond.
- Debenture bonds – Bonds which are not backed by a lien or mortgage. Also called an unsecured bond.
- Callable bonds – Bonds whose retirement is at the issuer's discretion.
- Convertible bonds – Bonds which grant the bondholder the choice of turning bonds into stock.

Bonds Payable, Required Disclosures, and Bond Issuance

- Bonds payable - A formal written promise to pay interest at specified intervals (usually semi-annually) and the principal amount at maturity. Bonds payable is a long term liability account showing the face, par, or maturity amount of bonds issued that remain outstanding as of the balance sheet date.

- Disclosure - Information about bonds must be disclosed on the balance sheet and in the notes to the financial statements. Amounts due in the next 12 months are presented as a current liability on the balance sheet. The remaining amount is presented as long-term. The fair value of the bonds must be disclosed in the notes to the financial statements, along with the method used to estimate the fair value. Other disclosures include: accounting policies, maturity dates, interest rates, conversion privileges, sinking fund requirements, off-balance-sheet credit risk or market risk, and other significant items.
- Bond Issuance – When a bond is issued, the face amount is recorded in the bonds payable account. If there is a premium or discount, it is noted in a separate account. When shown on the balance sheet, it can be a deduction or addition to the face amount of the bond.

Options

- Swap – The exchange of one stream of payments for another, usually entered into due to changes in investment objectives, maturities or quality.
- Swaption – When a swap has an option for the holder to enter into the swap in the future or extend or end the terms of an existing swap; essentially an option on a swap.
- Call option – An agreement or contract that gives the right to buy an underlying security at a specified price within a specific time period. Holders of call options profit when the price of the underlying asset goes up.
- Out of the money – When a call option is said to be out of the money, it means that the strike price is above the market value of the underlying. Put options are out of the money when the exercise price is below the underlying asset's market value. Also called underwater.
- Put option – An agreement or contract that gives the right to sell an underlying security at a specified price within a specific time period.

Distribution of Partnership Income and Loss

Typically, when a partnership is formed, there is a written contract outlining how the partnership income and loss are to be divided among the partners. The contract is known as a partnership agreement or a declaration of partnership. If there is no partnership agreement, income and loss is divided evenly between the partners. Situations which may cause difficulties in the division of income and loss include the following:

- If partners receive interest on capital balances, how the capital balances are created must be decided first. An example could be year-end amount or weighted average.
- Salaries for some or all of the partners. The partners decide if there are bonuses for some or all of the partners and if the bonus is dependent upon monies earned before or after salary and interest distributions.
- Remaining income needs to be addressed. The equation for the distribution is known as residual, remainder, or profit/loss sharing ratio. If the net income is inadequate for salaries, bonuses, and interest allocations, the amount should be addressed to create an equivalent negative remainder. The profit/loss sharing ratio then applies to the remainder unless it was decided that the losses should be handled in another way.

Change of Ownership in a Partnership and Partnership Liquidation

A change in ownership of a partnership, such as the addition of a new partner, retirement of a partner, or death of a partner, causes the original partnership to be dissolved. Under new ownership, the partnership business continues, and a new accounting unit must be set up. Prior to the new partnership accounting, the old accounts must be properly stated as to the date of the dissolution. If there is any income or loss, the partners' capital accounts should reflect the change, and all assets should be accounted for at fair market value, with liabilities at present value. The cause of the dissolution affects how the accounting adjustments are made. The dissolution is determined by two arrangements. The first occurs between the partnership and a partner. A new partner joins the partnership and contributes assets, or a partner leaves the partnership while taking assets. The second occurs between partners, such as if one partner buys an interest from one or more other partners, or if a retiring partner sells an interest to one or more partners. A partnership is liquidated when all the partnership's business transactions are completed and the business ceases to exist.

REVENUE RECOGNITION

Principles of revenue recognition are crucial to the GAAP requirement that accounting be done on the basis of accrual. A sum principle of revenue recognition is that revenues ought to be recognized when they are realized (or realizable) and earned—regardless of when any cash inflow is actually received. There can be accrued revenue, where revenue is earned prior to any cash inflow, and deferred revenue, where cash is received prior to the revenue's being earned. Revenue recognition also involves a number of more substantive and practical applications (e.g. whether revenue is earned on the date of sale or date of delivery for certain kinds of transactions), but the central principle is that revenues are recognized when earned.

COSTS, EXPENSES, AND EXPENDITURES

A cost generally refers to an outflow of cash but more specifically refers to the acquisition of an asset. An expense, on the other hand, generally refers to some cost that is paid in the context of a company's ordinary operations. For example, suppose that a clown purchased $100 worth of balloons, only $80 of which went towards the upcoming month's birthday parties where he would be working. In that case, there would be a $100 cost for the balloons acquired, $80 of which would be recorded as an expense (balloons utilized for his ordinary revenue-generating operations) and $20 of which would be recorded an *asset* (balloons for future use). When the clown later uses his $20 worth of balloons, the assets will decrease and the expenses will increase accordingly. An expenditure is any disbursement or payment doled out by the company, while an expense is specifically related to the outflow of economic benefits as part of a company's ordinary operations. Expenditures can serve many different purposes, including the acquisition of an asset, the decrease of a liability, or an expense itself. The expenditure refers simply to the fact of payment, while an expense is a payment for a specific purpose.

PREPAID EXPENSES

With accrual accounting, prepaid expenses are shown as assets when a business puts aside money early to pay for bills coming in the future. These expenses can be for insurance, rent, goods, or services. Prepaid expenses are generally classified as either current or noncurrent on the balance sheet, with current expenses being paid within a twelve-month period. When the asset is used to pay for the rent, insurance, or whatever else, then the asset account is credited and the expense account is debited with the proper amount.

EMPLOYEE COMPENSATION AND BENEFITS

Employee compensation is the sum total of repayment which a company provides its employees in exchange for their labor. It generally includes either wages or salary in addition to various benefits, such as paid time-off, insurance, or a company car. The monetary payment of employees can have guaranteed pay, most often in the form of a salary, and sometimes variable pay, which is payment based upon performance or results. Part of employee compensation sometimes equity compensation, where an employee can participate in the owning of the business as part of his repayment. The most common form of equity compensation is employee stock ownership plans (ESOPs).

Compensated Absences

Compensated absences refer to employees' time off—whether vacations, or holidays, or sick days—which still receives pay. The matching principle of accounting dictates that these expenses be recorded on the company's financial statements during the employee's course of working, rather than simply when the employee actually takes the time off. Each accounting period, the expense is debited (e.g., "compensated absences expense") and a corresponding liability is credited (e.g. "compensated absences payable"). Later, when the employee actually takes the time of compensated absence, the liability account is itself debited, not the expense account.

Deferred Compensation Arrangements

Deferred compensation arrangements are arrangements where an employee has earned compensation which will not be paid to him until a later date. Examples of deferred compensation arrangements are retirement plans (such as IRAs and 401(k)s) and stock option plans. A major advantage of such arrangements is that the taxes on the deferred compensation need not be paid until a later date; sometimes the deferred compensation will be taxed at a lower rate due to a lower future income.

Nonretirement Postemployment Benefits

Most postemployment benefits refer to the benefits which an employee receives once he retires, but there are a number of postemployment benefits which apply even to employees not yet in retirement. Examples of such nonretirement postemployment benefits are salary continuance, severance benefits, fringe benefits (like insurance), and disability-related benefits (like workers' compensation).

Properly Accounting for Compensated Absences and Postretirement Benefits

If (1) the payment of compensated absences and postretirement benefits is *probable*, (2) the amount is reasonably *estimable*, (3) the employee's service earning such benefits is *already rendered*, and (4) the employee's earned benefits involve *vested* rights (where the employer must compensate the employee even if his employment is terminated) or *accumulated* rights (where the benefits aggregate across periods), then the company ought to mark such benefits for employee compensation as a *liability*. Otherwise they ought to be recorded as contingencies.

Compensatory Employee Stock Purchase Plan

A compensatory employee stock purchase plan differs from a noncompensatory plan in that it does not have to meet any of the conditions that are set for the noncompensatory plan. Compensation assessment occurs, and the difference between what the employee pays and the market price at the measurement date is then divided amongst the relevant terms of the employee's services. The compensation cost is then acknowledged by the fair value method of option pricing. To be deemed an employee of the corporation, there must be an employer-employee relationship such that the employer has an acceptable amount of control over the individual. This means that besides the typical employee, the plan is now available to non-corporate members of the corporation's board of directors. Usually the measurement date is the date of the grant, but sometimes the measurement date is after the grant date. When this occurs, compensation costs are recorded and compiled for each period. The cost for the period is a function of the quoted market price at the end of the period, the approximate number of shares earned, and the option price.

Benefit Settlement and Curtailment

Benefit settlements are actions that cannot be altered alleviating the employer and/or the plan from its responsibility of commitment. The settlement causes the obligation risks to be relieved along with the assets that are used for the settlement. In addition to the settlement, there are gains and losses with earnings that must be noted. This amount has limitations such that it is either a *pro rata* share, or all, of the unrecognized gain or loss that is acknowledged when a settlement occurs. If a full settlement happens, then all the gains and losses are acknowledged. If only a partial settlement occurs, then the *pro rata* share is used on the notation of the unrecognized gain or loss. Curtailment notably lessens the expected years of the future service for current employees. It could also eliminate for a large number of employees, the accumulation of stated benefits or a portion or all of their future services. It is a loss from curtailment when unrecognized previous service cost is correlated with years of service that are not assumed to be carried out. The unrecognized previous service cost is the outstanding unrecognized net commitment at the date of the application of SFAS 87. With this particular action, projected benefit commitment can increase or decrease.

Properly Accounting for Income Taxes

A company arrives at its pretax income (sometimes called "pretax financial income," "book income," or other things) by subtracting its revenues from its expenses—keeping in mind that revenues are recognized when *earned* and expenses when *incurred*, rather than when the actual cash inflows or outflows occur. The income tax expense is then applied to the pretax income. If the expenses exceed the revenues, then the company will have a pretax financial loss but receive a tax refund or savings known as an income tax benefit. The main goals of income-tax accounting are to identity the income tax amount (or income tax benefit amount) and to properly recognize assets and liabilities which will be or have been grounds for tax deferral.

Transactions, Events, and Disclosures

Accounting Changes and Error Corrections

There are four classes of accounting changes: (1) changes in accounting principles (i.e. between different generally accepted principles), (2) changes in accounting estimates (due to new information or experience), (3) changes in a reporting entity (i.e., changes in what entity a business reports as), and (4) error corrections (e.g. from the recording of incorrect transactions, or from outright omission of records). The FASB has issued SFAS 154 to deal with issues regarding how companies should properly report these accounting changes.

AROs and Environmental Remediation Liabilities

Asset retirement obligations (AROs) are those obligations related to the future disposal of long-term assets—how such assets are retired by being dismantled, restored, or abandoned. When such long-term assets are first built or installed, the company needs to record an asset retirement cost (an asset) against an ARO (a liability). The asset becomes depreciated over time, the liability is accreted, and when the asset is finally retired, the actual expenses to retire the asset are recorded against the ARO. Environmental remediation liabilities are obligations of a company to perform some kind of clean-up or reparation of environmental damage. They are contingent liabilities, so their disclosure on a company's financial statements is contingent on a number of conditions, such as whether an actual environmental claim has been filed against the entity (by the EPA or a state agency) or whether it is probable that a relevant claim will be filed.

Business Combinations

A business combination is any consolidation of multiple businesses into one. There are three different kinds of business combination: (1) statutory mergers, where one company purchases all of another company's assets, leaving only the purchasing company to remain; (2) statutory consolidation, where two or more companies unite to form a new company which is itself a different existing entity from the previously-existing companies; and (3) stock acquisition, where one company purchases the majority of another company's stock, but both companies continue as economic entities.

Acquisition Method

According to the acquisition method, the acquiring company ought to recognize all the identifiable assets, liabilities, and equity obtained in its acquisition, including noncontrolling interest. For assets to qualify as identifiable, they must be capable of participating in discrete transactions or otherwise exist as a result of contractual or other legal rights. The acquiring company must then measure the acquired assets, liabilities, and noncontrolling interest according to their fair values as of the acquisition date. In addition, the acquiring company needs to recognize and measure goodwill or a gain from a bargain purchase and disclose the details of the acquisition in the notes to the financial statements.

Accounting for Investment of a Company in Another Business

The three ways for a corporation to account for investment in another business are:

- Cost Method – If the amount invested amounts to 20% or less of common stock, giving the corporation negligible influence over the business, then this method should be used. When a dividend is received, it is noted as income and the investment meets the requirements set forth by SFAS 115.

- Equity Method – When the amount invested equals 20-50% of the outstanding common stock, then the investor has a meaningful influence over the business and the equity method is appropriate. The equity method has the cash dividends reducing the carrying amount of investment and the income is the *pro rata* share of the business's earnings.
- Consolidated Financial Statements – Required by Accounting Research Bulletin (ARB) 51 when a corporation owns more than 50% of a company's common or voting stock. SFAS 141 on business combinations documents standards for accounting and reporting.

Off-Balance Sheet Transactions, VIEs, and Noncontrolling Interests

An off-balance-sheet transaction is any business arrangement which, whether or not it affects the company materially, is structured so as not to appear on the company's balance sheet. Ordinarily, off-balance sheet transactions are utilized to reduce a company's apparent debt and thereby improve its debt-to-equity and leverage ratios. A variable-interest entity (VIE) is an entity in which an investor holds a controlling interest which does not consist of enough voting privileges to result in a majority. A noncontrolling interest (also known as a minority interest) is a limited ownership stake in a business where one has less than 50% of the total outstanding shares. This prevents one from controlling the business's operations.

Companies always must consolidate their financial statements with any subsidiaries in which they possess a controlling interest. This helps users of the financial statements to see all the relevant information without important data being concealed in off-balance sheet transactions. In addition, there are conditions when a business may need to consolidate its financial statements even without having a controlling interest constituted by majority voting rights in the company (VIE). This all is to ensure the transparent communication of the parent company's activities.

Consolidation

If a company owns over 50% of another company's voting stock, it generally is required to produce consolidated financial statements for the two firms. The only exception to this is when control of the subsidiary does not rest with the parent, despite the parent's having majority voting rights. Examples of such an exception are when the company is in bankruptcy or is operating under strict government regulations which place doubt on the parent's ability to control the firm. Otherwise, all subsidiaries are required to be consolidated, even if the parent and subsidiary companies have different fiscal years, and the financial data (e.g. revenues and expenses) shall be recorded from the subsidiary only from the point of consolidation, not prior. To execute the consolidation properly, all capital and investment accounts, intercompany balances, and intercompany transactions need to be eliminated.

Contingencies and Commitments

Commitments are arrangements where a company agrees and intends to perform some action in the future. When disclosing commitments, a company ought to specify the nature and amount of the commitment as well as any peculiarities or uncertainties related to it.

Contingencies are circumstances which involve possible loss as dependent (contingent) upon the occurrence of future events. Accounting problems related to contingencies deal with the probability of the future event's occurrence and the estimated amount to be paid for the contingency.

EPS

Earnings per share (EPS) is the earnings amount which can be attributed to each share of common stock (that is, preferred stock are excluded), and is generally the most important factor in the determination of share price. It is calculated by subtracting the company's preferred dividends from its net income and dividing that total by the average outstanding shares. Since EPS is concerned only with a company's net income without regard to how the income is produced, it is not completely determinative of the worth of a share. Specifically, if one company can generate the same EPS as another but will less debt, then that company is more efficient with what it possesses.

Basic Earnings per Share and Diluted Earnings per Share

Basic earnings per share is the standard or default form of earnings per share: it calculates the net income of a company (less preferred dividends) for each share of common stock outstanding. On the other hand, diluted earnings per share is the earnings per share which would be calculated if all stock options, warrants, preferred stock, and convertible bonds were exercised. Diluted earnings per share is, in essence what basic earnings per share would be in a worst-case scenario—where the number of outstanding shares are the highest they could be.

Disposal Activities and Discontinued Operations

A disposal activity is any action of a company to dispense of a long-term asset. Whenever a company does this and receives a different amount of money than the book value (i.e. carrying value), the company should report a gain or loss on that asset as a separate income statement item. Then, since sales of long-term assets are supposed to be recorded as investing activities in the statement of cash flows, whereas income statement items are to be recorded as operating activities, there is the problem of double-counting these transactions. To solve this, the company should reduce their net income for any gains and increase it for any losses on such sales. Discontinued operations are contrasted from the firm's continuing operations. They are operations of whole divisions, subsidiaries, or segments of a business which the company intends (specifically and formally) to terminate from the company. Revenues and expenses for discontinued operations are reported separately on the income statement near the end.

Going-Concern Issues

Business failure is devastating to shareholders, lenders, and other stakeholders in a business, making the detection of signs of looming business failure paramount. If there is doubt that a business will be a **going concern**—that it will apparently persist into the indefinite future—CPAs are required to disclose this in the company's financial statements. CPAs must resist pressures from company officers or directors to refrain from disclosing important going-concern items or even to delay the financial statements' issuance so that the going-concern issue can then be corrected.

Fair Value Measurements, Disclosures, and Reporting

Fair value is the price at which an asset or liability would be exchanged in the marketplace between willing and able buyers acting rationally and without bias. To measure the initial fair value for some item, one should consider the transaction price and determine what differences there might be between the transaction price and the fair value. For example, if a transaction is made between related parties or in an unusual market, the transaction price would differ from the fair value of the item. The company should disclose its valuation techniques for determining fair value in its footnotes, in addition to any other pertinent details; and it should report any unrealized gains or losses on items according to their fair value.

Financial Instruments and Derivative Instruments

A financial instrument can be cash or proof of ownership in a business. It could also be a contractual obligation that makes one business required to pay cash or equivalent to another business when the two businesses are not on good terms. Another financial instrument is a contractual right, which means a business is obligated to receive cash (or an equivalent) from another business, or it can exchange the cash or equivalent on good terms with that business.

A derivative instrument is a contract that meets three specific requirements.

1. It has at least an underlying and notional amount or payment provision.
2. It maintains a zero or small investment.
3. The derivative instrument allows for a net settlement. The instrument can be easily settled outside of the contract or by receipt of the asset.

When the value of a financial instrument comes from something not part of the financial instrument itself, then it is a derivative instrument. An underlying is a financial or physical variable with changes that can be observed or objectively verified. Examples include interest rates, commodity prices, exchange rates, a business's credit rating, rainfall, or temperature changes. The number of units pertaining to the derivative instrument is called the notional amount. Bushels of wheat or shares of stock are two examples of notional amounts. The underlying and the notional amount are necessary to prove whether the financial instrument is a derivative instrument and the outcome amount of the derivative instrument.

Hybrid Instruments, Embedded Derivative Instrument, and Bifurcation

- Hybrid instrument – A financial instrument that contains components that, if taken by themselves, would be a derivative instrument.
- Embedded derivative instrument – What is contained in a "host contract" of a hybrid instrument.
- Bifurcation – A process which separates the embedded derivative instrument from the host contract and enables the embedded derivative to be treated as a stand-alone instrument. When this occurs, the host contract is treated in a normal accounting manner and the embedded derivative instrument is considered a stand-alone derivative instrument.

Underlying, Notional Amount, Fair Market Value, and Hedging

An underlying is a financial or physical variable that specifies an amount, such as interest rate, security price, or foreign exchange rates. An underlying may be a price or rate of an asset or liability but is not the asset or liability itself. A notional amount is an amount of currency, e.g. dollars or pounds, or other element, such as bushels or shares, that is specified in a contract. Fair market value is the price that is mutually acceptable between two unrelated parties without either being forced or coerced into making the transaction. Hedging is a financial strategy that attempts to reduce risk or afford some protection against the risk involved when prices rise and fall. One financial instrument counterbalances another.

Hedging Instruments

The two conditions necessary for a derivative instrument to be classified as a hedging instrument are:

- As a minimum, the following must be substantiated:
    - Objective and strategy of the hedge
    - Hedging instrument and hedged item
    - On a go-forward basis, a determination of the effectiveness of the hedge

- The determination of the effectiveness of the hedge instrument is quantified by its ability to generate changes in fair value that offset changes in the value of the hedged item. This effectiveness must continue throughout its life and have high correlation to the risk. It also must be measured a minimum of four times per year and when earnings or financial statements are made. To be "highly effective," the hedging instrument's cumulative change should be between 80% and 125% of the inverse cumulative changes in the fair value or cash flows of hedged item.

Required Financial Statement Disclosures with Respect to Both Derivative and Nonderivative Financial Instruments Used as Hedging Instruments

As amended by SFAS 161 in March 2008, required financial statement disclosure with respect to derivative and nonderivative financial instruments that are used as hedging instruments include:

1. Objectives and strategies for using derivatives by primary underlying risk and accounting designation (for example, interest rate, credit, foreign exchange rate, or overall price) to better convey the purpose of derivative use in terms of the risks that the entity is intending to manage
2.
    a. the location and fair values of derivative instruments in the statement of financial position and
    b. the location and amount of gains and losses on derivative instruments in the statement of financial performance in tabular format
3. Information about credit-risk-related contingent features to explain the potential effect on an entity's liquidity from using derivative
4. Cross-referencing within the footnotes to help users locate information about derivative instruments

Whenever a financial statement is prepared, a disclosure must also be reported on each type of hedge. Even if it is not a hedging instrument, derivative instruments must also follow the disclosure guidelines.

Fair Value Hedge

When a derivative instrument is used to hedge the risk of changes in the fair value of an asset or liability, it is a fair value hedge. All or a portion of the hedged item must be of a recognized asset or liability or of an unrecognized firm commitment. An example of this occurs in foreign currency transactions. When it involves an unrecognized firm commitment, three criteria must be met. The first criterion is that the commitment is binding between both parties. The second is that all the important terms are clearly defined and the third is that a nonperformance clause is included that gives more reason for the performance to be completed. Hedged assets' or liabilities' gains or losses, and the hedging instrument itself must be recognized in current earnings under SFAS 133.

Accounting for Cash Flow Hedges

The effective portion of a hedging instrument is recorded in other comprehensive income (OCI) under SFAS 133. The ineffective portion, which may include excluded components, is recorded on a cumulative basis depending on whichever is smaller, the cumulative gain or loss on the derivative since the hedge was initiated or the cumulative gain or loss from the change in expected cash flows from the hedged instrument since the hedge was initiated. Adjustments need to be made if reclassifications occur with other comprehensive income to current earnings. An example is when hedged inventory is sold and the cost of the inventory is recorded as cost of goods sold.

Foreign Currency Transactions and Translation

A foreign currency transactions is any transaction denominated in a currency different from the company's own functional currency. Since exchange rates can differ from day to day, there can be fluctuations resulting in a higher or lower inflow or outflow than originally expected. These should be marked accordingly by the company as gains and losses and reported as other comprehensive income (OCI), since they are not part of the ordinary operations of the business. Sometimes, to avoid the effects of foreign-currency fluctation, companies will hedge their transactions with contractual provisions specifying the precise exchange rate (or the day corresponding to an exchange rate) for the terms of the transaction.

Foreign Currency Denominated Forecasted Transactions and Net Investments in Foreign Operations

Foreign currency denominated forecasted transactions can only use derivative instruments marked as such. An example would be when a price is denominated in foreign currency in a forecasted export sale. Forecasted transactions differ from firm commitments in that the cash flow timings are questionable. This variability causes the hedging instrument to be recorded as cash flow hedges. Hedge accounting is permissible with unrelated associates. It can also be used in certain cases with intercompany exchanges.

Net investments in foreign operations – In addition to the standards set forth in SFAS 52, the hedging instrument must be deemed "highly effective." The balance sheet will reflect the changes in the fair value of the hedging instrument in the other comprehensive income section and the accumulated other comprehensive income account in the equity section.

Foreign Currency Hedges, Unrecognized Firm Commitment, and Available-for-Sale Securities

Foreign currency hedges – Businesses engaging in normal business transactions involving assets or liabilities that have foreign currency denominations often offset the risks with forward exchange contracts, creating a true hedge.

Unrecognized firm commitment – This occurs when a derivative instrument or a nonderivative financial instrument is used as a hedge with characteristics depending upon variability in foreign currency exchange rates. It can be considered a fair value hedge if those standards are achieved.

Available-for-sale securities – Derivative instruments can be utilized as a hedge to debt or equity for these types of securities. Additional standards must be fulfilled for equity securities:

- The investor's normal currency cannot be used as the exchange denomination in a trade.
- The same foreign currency must be used for the dividends and the sale of the security.

Conditions and Objectives of Foreign Currency Translation

The translation of foreign currency into US dollars typically occurs when these two conditions apply.

- When foreign currency transactions are in a denomination other than the business's normal currency.
- When the financial statements of branches, divisions, subsidiaries, or other investees are in foreign currency and must be combined, consolidated, or assimilated using the equity method into the financial statements of a US business.

The objectives of foreign currency translation are:

- To give details on projected economic effects of rate exchanges on the business's cash flows and equity.
- To give details on consolidated financial statements correlating the financial results to the individual foreign consolidated business as shown by the normal currency of each reporting business.

Functional Currency, Local Currency, Reporting Currency, Translation Adjustments, and Remeasurement

Functional currency is the currency or medium of exchange of the dominant economic environment where the business operates. This is the medium that the business uses in day-to-day operations to generate and expend cash. Local currency applies to the medium of exchange in a particular country. Reporting currency is the currency or medium of exchange that a business utilizes when preparing its financial statements. Translation adjustments appear when financial statements are translated from the business's functional currency into its reporting currency. Remeasurement arises when a business keeps its accounting records in a different currency than its functional currency. Monetary balances must be translated using current exchange rates, while nonmonetary balances use historical exchange rates for remeasurement purposes.

Impairment

Impairment occurs when the fair value of a long-lived asset is less than its book value (i.e. carrying value)—when the asset is recorded on the books at a higher value than it is really worth. Impaired assets can fall into three categories: assets held for sales, assets held for use, and assets held for disposal other than by sale.

Indefinite Useful Life and Impairment Loss

If an intangible asset does not have any legal, regulatory, contractual, competitive, or economic considerations that put restrictions on its useful life, then it is deemed to have an indefinite useful life. This should not be confused with infinite. The asset must be tested annually for impairment.

To account for goodwill with respect to an intangible asset, an impairment method must be used as opposed to an amortization method. SFAS 142 states that intangible assets are not considered wasting assets and provides clear instructions on testing for impairment. At least once a year, the fair market value is compared with the documented value of the intangible asset. If for some reason the carrying amount is not recoverable or if the carrying amount is greater than the fair market value, then a loss must be recognized. The new carrying amount is used from that time forward. If the impairment loss is somehow reversed, it cannot be recognized.

Goodwill Impairment Testing and Reporting Unit

Goodwill must be tested for impairment at least annually using a two-step process that begins with an estimation of the fair value of a reporting unit. The first step is a screen for potential impairment, and the second step measures the amount of impairment, if any. If certain criteria are met, the requirement to test goodwill for impairment annually can be satisfied without a remeasurement of the fair value of a reporting unit. A reporting unit is a unit of the combined entity into which an acquired entity is integrated, and is defined as an operating segment or one level below an operating segment (referred to as a component).

TWO-LEVEL IMPAIRMENT TEST FOR GOODWILL

The two levels of impairment testing for goodwill are:

- The first level determines if there are differences in the reporting unit's fair market value and its carrying amount plus goodwill. If the fair market value is greater than the carrying amount, then the goodwill is not impaired. The second level is not required.
- If the carrying amount is greater than the fair market value, then the second level becomes necessary. An impairment loss is documented if the carrying amount is greater than the implied fair market value of the goodwill. The loss cannot be larger than the goodwill's carrying amount. When the loss is documented, the new carrying amount of goodwill is now used as the financial basis. It cannot ever be reversed.

CATEGORIES OF IMPAIRED LONG-LIVED ASSETS

The three categories for impaired long-lived assets are:

- Held for sale – To meet this requirement, the asset must be available for sale and the sale to be completed within a year. The value of the asset is the lower of book value and fair market value minus expenses for selling the asset. The asset is no longer depreciated.
- Assets held for use – In order for the business to be able to recognize the impaired asset, its undiscounted cash flows must be less than the book value. The loss is determined by the difference between the book value and fair market value.
- Disposal other than by sale – If a long-lived asset is to be deserted, traded for a comparable asset, or given to a subsidiary, then the asset is to be treated accordingly. Appropriate corrections need to be made to the depreciable life of the asset if it is cast-off. When the asset is traded or given away to a subsidiary, the loss is documented if the book value is greater than the fair market value.

INTERIM FINANCIAL REPORTING

The term interim reporting is used for financial reports that do not cover one year. Interim reporting provides more timely information than annual reports and enables the company to give greater detail on significant business issues that may be lost in an annual report. APB 28 describes the GAAP requirements for interim reporting. Two methods for interim reporting are:

- Discrete view – The interim report covers a specific accounting period and must abide by the same principles and procedures as an annual report.
- Integral view – Breaks down the annual period into integral parts each of which has an interim report. This is the FASB preferred method. The interim report should show special accruals, deferrals, and allocations utilized, all of which are expectations in the annual report.

LEASE

LEASE, LESSOR, LESSEE, AND LEASE TERM

A lease is an agreement or contract regarding the right to use property, plant, or equipment for a certain period of time. If the lease gives a substantial portion of the benefits and risks that corresponds to the ownership of the property to the person obtaining the lease, it should be recorded as an asset and a liability by that person. The person leasing the property records the transaction like a sale or financing agreement. The remaining types of leases should be recorded as operating leases. The lessor is the person or business that leases the property, plant, equipment, or other asset. The lessee is the person or business that is able to utilize the asset and makes payments for that privilege to the lessor. The lease term is the fixed, noncancelable period of the lease in addition to:

- All periods as described in bargain renewal options.
- All periods where there is not a renewal of the lease by the lessee, if a penalty occurs which makes renewal practically guaranteed.
- All periods before the date of exercisable bargain purchase options.
- All periods that may renew or extend the lease terms at the lessor's discretion.

LEASEHOLD AND LEASEHOLD IMPROVEMENT

A leasehold is a right given to use rental property for a specific time period. When entering into this type of agreement, usually the first and last year's rental amount is required in cash. The last year's cash amount is accounted for as leasehold and remains an intangible asset until the final year, when it becomes a rental expense. Leasehold improvement occurs when the business that rents the property makes improvements to the property that are valuable beyond the time period in which they are made. Those improvements become part of the leased property and are owned by the lessor at the end of the lease period. The costs are capitalized over the useful life or time remaining in the lease, whichever is shorter. If the time on the lease agreement is extended, the capitalized amount should also cover the extended time.

MINIMUM LEASE PAYMENTS

Minimum lease payments (MLPs) are payments or required payments correlating to leased property. The MLP does not include executory costs. If the contract contains a bargain purchase option (BPO), minimum payments are required for the term of the lease and it includes the bargain purchase price. If not, the MLP takes into account the following:

- Minimum rental payments as defined by the lease for the lease term.
- Any guarantee of a remaining value of the leased asset at the end of the lease by the lessee.
- If the lessee does not renew the lease, then any agreed-upon penalty payment.
- The lessor may require a guarantee of the remaining amount by a third party, in addition to minimum lease payments, if the third party is financially capable of releasing its obligations.
- The MLP does not include managerial costs that are paid by the lessor or lessee, or unexpected rentals.

CAPITAL LEASE AND OPERATING LEASE WITH RESPECT TO THE LESSEE

To be able to qualify as a capital lease, the lease must meet one of the following four conditions.

- Transfer of ownership to the lessee at the end of the lease period.
- A bargain purchase option in the lease.
- The term of the lease covers at least 75% or more of the commercial life of the leased property.
- The present value of the minimum lease payments, less executory expenses, is equal to or greater than 90% of the fair value of the leased property at the time the lease is initiated. An exception to this rule is if there is less than 25% of the commercial life remaining, in which case the lease can be a capital lease if it meets the first or second condition.

Operating lease – All leases that do not meet the conditions for a capital lease. All recording must document that it is an operating lease.

Executory Costs

Executory costs include insurance, maintenance, and taxes that must be paid on the asset during its fiscal life. The type of payments is periodic and should be accounted for when paid or accrued by the lessor or lessee. If the obligation to pay is with the lessor, then the part of the minimum lease payments representing the executory costs should be taken off of the lessee's minimum lease payments. If the obligation to pay is with the lessee, then the executory payments should not be part of the minimum lease payments. The expenses should be recorded in the proper expense accounts.

Guaranteed and Unguaranteed Residual Value

The estimated fair value of the leased property at the end of the lease term is its residual value.

- Guaranteed – When there is a specific amount payable when the lease has ended.
- It may be a purchase payment for the leased property or an amount to make up for a deficit between a preset amount that the lessee guarantees and the realization of the property.
- The guaranteed residual value is included in the minimum lease payments for the lessor and the lessee.
- Unguaranteed – When there is not a specified amount guaranteed by the lessee or a third party related to the lessee.
- The unguaranteed residual value is not included in the minimum lease payments by the lessor or the lessee.
- The sum of the minimum lease payments and the unguaranteed residual value is the lessor's gross investment in the lease.

Recording a Capital Lease from the Lessee's Perspective

The lessee documents the lower of the fair value of the leased property when the lease is initiated or the present value of the minimum lease payments, calculated by the present value discount rate when recording a capital lease. The amount is recorded as an asset under "Leased Asset Under Capital Leases" and as a liability under "Obligations Under Capital Leases." If the annual rental is payable at the beginning of the year, the component for the present value of annuity in advance is used to calculate the present value of the minimum lease payments. If the annual rental is payable at the end of the year, the component for the present value of ordinary annuity is used.

Amortization of Capital Leases from the Lessee's Perspective

Leased capital property should be subject to the same depreciation method as comparable owned assets.

- Amortize over remaining estimated economic life – If the lease meets either of the first two criteria for a capital lease (the lease transfers ownership of the property to the lessee at the end of the lease or the contract contains a bargain purchase option), then the asset must be amortized over the remaining economic life by the lessee.
- Amortize over lease term – If the lease meets either of the second two criteria for capital leases (the term is 75% or more of the economic life or the present value of the minimum lease payments is equal to or greater than 90% of the fair value of the leased property when the lease was formed), it is categorized as a capital lease and should be amortized over the lease term, not the life of the asset.
- Amortize to expected residual value – If the capital lease includes transfer of ownership, the leased asset should be amortized by the lessee to the expected residual amount if there is one at the end of the lease agreement.

Documentation of Lease Liability

Effective interest method – Used to amortize the lease liability.

Allocation of lease payments – Each lease payment is divided between interest expense and the lease debt. The payments cause a decrease in interest expense and in the amount of the total lease debt. The payment amount should never be reported as a rent expense.

Amortization rate – While the same present value amount is used in recording the asset and liability balances at the beginning of the lease term, the balances will be amortized at different rates over the life of the asset or the term of the lease.

Disclosure with Respect to the Lessee

Lessee lease disclosures include:

- Capital leases – With a capital lease, it is mandatory that the lessee disclose the gross amount of assets as of the date of each balance sheet by the major classifications of function or nature. The lessee must also disclose the present value of future minimum lease payments as of the date of the latest balance sheet documented both as a total and for each of the five succeeding fiscal years.
- Operating leases with initial or remaining noncancelable terms in excess of 1 year – the lessee is required to disclose a routine description of the leasing agreement with the future minimum rental payments in total and for each of the next five years.

Operating Leases

If the three conditions for a sales-type or direct financing type of lease are not fulfilled and the four criteria for a capital lease are also not met, then the lease is known as an operating lease. This type of lease does not have a transfer of risks and benefits of ownership, nor does it have the property transferred on the accounting records of the lessor to the lessee. The balance sheet of the lessor records the information with the property, plant, and equipment. The lease agreement spells out the recognition of rent over the period of the lease for the lessee and the lessor. For the lessee, it is an expense that becomes payable. For the lessor, it is revenue that becomes a receivable. Normal depreciation methods are used by the lessor for the leased property. Costs incurred with the initiation of the lease, such as commission or legal fees, are calculated by the straight-line method and spread out over the term of the lease. If there are any executory costs, they are recognized when they occur as expenses. If the lessor received rent in advance, it should be recorded as deferred revenue and accounted for when appropriate. The lessor must also comply with SFAS 144, by having a leased asset meet the impairment test for long-lived assets. Executory costs, amortization of initial direct costs, depreciation, amortization of any lease bonus, and periodic rental payments all determine the net rental income accounted for by the lessor for the operating lease.

Classification of Financial Instruments as Liability or Equity

While the distinction between liabilities (ownership by another) and equity (ownership by the owners of a company) is easy to categorize, sometimes it can be difficult to apply, particularly to financial instruments. Since different classifications of these financial instruments can greatly affect a company's measurement of performance (such as its debt-to-equity ratio), the classification the company utilizes is significant. There are three different approaches to this classification: the basic ownership approach, the ownership-settlement approach, and the re-assessed expected outcomes approach.

Nonmonetary Transactions

Nonmonetary transactions are transactions which do not result in any fund transfer between or among accounts. They can be reciprocal, where two parties each transfer a nonmonetary good, service, or asset; or they can be nonreciprocal, where one party transfers one unilaterally. An exchange of equivalent assets (usually determined according to the assets' fair values), such as machinery for inventory, would constitute a reciprocal nonmonetary transaction; and a donation of physical inventory from one organization to another would constitute a nonreciprocal nonmonetary transaction. There are some nonmonetary transactions, however, when the ordinary accounting guidance for nonmonetary transactions does not apply. This occurs, for example, in exchanges of one business for another, of nonmonetary assets between commonly-controlled parties, of assets for an ownership interest, and of financial assets.

The following rules apply when nonmonetary assets are exchanged between two business entities.

- As part of the conservative approach, losses are always documented.
- If there is a positive difference in the fair market value to one business, it is required to show the gain.
- When conditions for fair market value cannot be met, it is necessary to utilize the book value of the asset being transferred. If boot is given as part of the exchange, it becomes part of the asset's recorded book value with the asset's transferred value. When boot is received, a portion of the amount is recorded as a gain.

Typically, fair market values are used with exchanges of property, equipment, or inventory. If the value of one of the transferable properties cannot be determined, then the fair market value of the other property is used for both. An exception to this procedure could be that the fair market value cannot be established. The fair market value is not used when the exchange is used to promote sales or if it does not have any business foundation.

Related Parties and Related-Party Transactions

Related parties are any parties who hold some sort of special relationship without any transactions having been made between them. These special relationships can be with family members of employees or management, significant shareholders in the company, company executives, and others. Since these relationships have the potential to create conflicts of interest where the related parties are benefited but not the company as a whole (and thus the shareholders), companies are required to disclose all their related-party transactions on their Form 10-K.

Research and Development

The term research includes expenditures that are associated with pertinent knowledge that leads to developing or improving a product or process. Development costs involve the transition from research into a new product or process or improving a product or process. Examples of costs related to research and development:

- Laboratory research
- Concept design or prototype
- Alternative designs or processes
- Testing of the design, prototype, or process
- Modification of the design, prototype, or process
- The tools, dyes, or molds required for the new design, prototype, or process
- Engineering for the final design, prototype, or process

Examples of costs which are not related to research and development:

- Engineering costs after initial production run
- Quality control and initial product testing costs
- Troubleshooting problems during production
- Specific customer requested modifications
- Seasonal adaptations
- Regular design and maintenance for production
- Patents
- Construction setup and equipment for new plants

Factors of Consideration When Accounting for Research and Development Costs

Since it is difficult to predict with any certainty how research and development will provide economic benefits in the future, nearly all research and development costs need to be expensed when they are incurred. This includes any facilities, equipments, materials, and other assets which have no use except for a particular research and development project; all of them should be expensed when acquired. But for those things which are intended to have other uses (whether in other research and development, or in the company's ordinary profit-generating operations), they should be recorded as assets.

Segment Reporting

Segment reporting highlights risks and returns, showing financial position and performance by segment, and is used by companies that provide groups of products or services or operate in diverse geographical areas. SFAS 131 sets the standards for reporting on different components of a business's operations, products and services, geographic areas, and largest customers. The focus of the reporting is to give prospective investors or lenders information about the future of the company. The segment report gives details on trends, opportunities, and risk factors that are usually summarized in consolidated statements.

Another important feature of the segment report is the ability to document "intersegment transactions" which are not found in consolidated statements. SFAS 131 requires the documentation to reflect how a manager would organize segments to make operating decisions and assess performance. The reports can also be set up by products or services, by geography, by type of customer, etc. When using the management approach to reporting, consistent information on the business is readily available for internal and external reporting and enables those reports to be correlated. SFAS 131 is not for non-profit or nonpublic business entities.

Reportable Segments

Reportable segments are operating segments that must pass at least one of the 10% tests of SFAS 131. Another test is the 75% test, which allows combinations of segments to be reported together if their totals are greater than 75% of the sum of the revenues, be it unaffiliated, intersegment, or total, or operating profit or loss, or segment assets. A business may also combine operating segments if they are in similar economic situations and are alike in the following ways:

- Type of products and services.
- Type of production processes.
- Customer for their products or services.
- Means of distribution for products or preparations in services.
- Regulatory environment.

The combination reports do not have to meet the 10% test, but if the business does this for an operating report, the segments should fulfill most of the combination requirements stated. If the business chooses to do the combination operating report without the 10% criteria, it may also report on each segment alone as opposed to a total report.

Operating Segments

The definition of operating segments, per SFAS 131 is:

"A component of an enterprise engaged in business activity for which it may earn revenues and incur expenses, about which separate financial information is available that is evaluated regularly by the chief operating decision makers in deciding how to allocate resources and in assessing performance."

To be a reportable segment, one of three 10% tests must be fulfilled.

- Revenues – The segment revenue, including intersegment revenue, is 10% or more of combined segment revenue also with intersegment revenue.
- Operating profit or loss – The total amount of segment profit or loss is 10% or more of the larger in total amount of combined profit for segments reporting profit or combined loss for segments reporting loss.
- Segment assets – The segment's assets are 10% or more of total segment assets.

Segment Disclosures Required by SFAS 131

SFAS 131 requires that segment disclosures incorporate the following:

- General information – The business's reportable segments, with notes on whether or not operating segments have been combined, must be defined by management. The explanation by management should also give details on types of products and services correlating to each reportable segment with revenues.
- Reconciliations – The segment figures and the reported corresponding business figures must be reconciled.
- Interim period information – Typically, interim disclosures are not as detailed as in the annual financial report, but some segment disclosures are necessary to interim financial reports.

Software Costs

A primary question with accounting for software costs is whether to treat computer software as an intangible asset or as property, plant, and equipment. Generally speaking, software costs are classified as intangible assets due to their non-physical nature, but there are certain occasions when they may be classified as property, plant, and equipment. If software will be utilized in the production of goods and services, such as for a software company, then it meets the criteria of property, plant, and equipment and can be classified accordingly. But if the software is utilized to more efficiently track and monitor the company's operations, then it should not be treated as property, plant, and equipment.

Subsequent Events

Subsequent events are any events which occur between the balance sheet date and the date when financial statements are issued or able to be issued. (They can therefore be called "post-balance-sheet events.") Examples of these events are lawsuits and asset impairments. Sometimes these events require the modification of balance sheet items and income statement items before the year-end date, but some will not. Among those that will not, they should be disclosed by the company in the notes to their financial statements if the events are significant.

Derecognition of Assets and Liabilities

The derecognition of an asset or liability is simply its being removed, whether in part or in whole, from the balance sheet. Accounting questions regarding derecognition typically arise in the context of financial instruments, especially with respect to special-purpose entities and whether or not financial statements ought to be consolidated. The IASB has provided much guidance on the accounting for recognition and derecognition in IAS 39, *Financial Instruments: Recognition and Measurement.*

Activities Associated with Servicing of Financial Assets

Usually included in the transfer of assets, servicing can be listed on its own if it is separated by contract from the financial asset. Activities typically associated with the servicing of financial assets are:

- Collection of payments
- Payment of taxes and insurance
- Monitoring of delinquent accounts
- Foreclosures
- Investments
- Accounting

Servicing is generally deemed a benefit, as it is highly compensated through fees, late charges, float, or additional income. If for some reason the fees, charges, etc., do not compensate for the servicing of the assets, then they become liabilities. Service liabilities usually have a negative impact on the sale of the asset. The servicing contract is deemed more than adequate, adequate, or less than adequate with respect to its compensation and if it is an asset or liability.

Recording of the Fair Market Value Process for Servicing Assets and Liabilities

This begins with the fair market value of the servicing asset and servicing liability. The value is then assessed at each recording period. When a change occurs in the fair market value, it is recorded in the earnings for that time period. Also, required reporting for each time period on the income statement are disclosures represented by management's judgment in determining its classes, its risks, how changes and their reporting in income statement affects fair market value changes, and agreed-upon servicing fees, late fees, and extraneous fees. Beginning and ending balances, additions, disposals, changes in fair market value technique used, and changes in fair market value must be revealed. It should also be noted what fair market value technique was used and information pertaining to details on the model used.

Recording of the Amortization Process for Servicing Assets and Liabilities

This begins with the fair market value of the servicing asset and servicing liability. Next the assets are amortized proportionately and periodically based on net servicing income or loss. The assets are evaluated periodically for impairment or increases in fair market value. The type and magnitude of risk is used to separate, evaluate, and measure impairment of assets. The impairment is then documented in a valuation allowance account, which also reflects changes as necessary. Liabilities are also amortized proportionately and periodically based on net servicing loss. If the fair market value is greater than the book value through the changes, then the liability should be increased and the loss recorded. The disclosures with this method need to include beginning and ending balances, additions, disposals, amortizations, valuation allowance marking adjustments of carrying value, non-temporary impairments, and other balance adjustments. The documentation should also record how these determinations were made with respect to valuation techniques, model assumptions, and measurements for impairment.

Governmental Accounting and Reporting

Government Accounting vs. For-Profit Business Accounting

Governmental accounting differs from for-profit business accounting as follows:

- There is not a profit goal. An exception to this could be a government utility.
- Legality prevails over restrictions in raising and spending of revenues.
- There is not a means to correlate revenues and expenditures one-to-one because revenues are from people other than those receiving the services.
- Public officials are given the role of overseers of accountability of resources.
- There are documents relating to fund accounting and reporting and government-wide reporting.
- Some funds must document their budgets.
- Some funds may use modified accrual accounting instead of full accrual accounting.

The regulations behind state and local government reporting come from the Governmental Accounting Standards Board, GASB.

Basis of Governmental Accounting

In governmental accounting, the accounting basis to be utilized is contingent upon the nature of the funds accounted for. There is a modified accrual basis to be used for governmental fund type statements (e.g. general revenue, special revenue, capital projects), which accrues revenues when they are available and measurable, and which treats fixed assets as expenditures. There is also an ordinary accrual basis to be used for proprietary fund statements, where revenues are accrued as earned and where fixed assets are capitalized. The accrual basis is also generally used for fiduciary fund statements.

Fund Accounting Concepts and Applications

Fundamental to fund accounting are the basic distinctions among types of funds in governmental accounting. There are three main types of funds:

- Governmental funds are utilized to fund general activities like the police department, the fire department, the courts, and general administration. The accounting equation for most governmental funds is (Current Assets – Current Liabilities = Fund Balance).
- Proprietary funds are utilized to fund activities which government entities need to undertake in order to continue functioning as normal; these activities are ones which businesses tend to undertake as well, such as utilities. Accounting for proprietary funds seeks to keep track of all relevant assets and liabilities, some simply current assets and liabilities.
- Fiduciary funds are those funds which the government holds either as a trustee or as an agent—referred to as trust funds and agency funds, respectively. These funds can be related to pensions, investment, and private purposes.

Budgetary Accounting

Since governmental organizations are funded by taxation, they are therefore on a budget, which their accounting must accordingly reflect. Budgetary accounting shows a particular regard for future planning in addition to past reporting, anticipating budgetary inflows as well as planned expenditures and acquisitions. This might include encumbrances, which are obligations to spend money in the future (not liabilities, however) recorded in order to prevent the depletion of available budgetary funds.

CAFR

A comprehensive annual financial report (CAFR) is a governmental financial report which all US governmental entities must publicly disclose. It has an introductory section, a financial section, and a statistical section. The introductory section contains the independent auditor's report (if available), the letter of transmittal, and other material. The financial section contains management's discussion and analysis, financial statements with footnotes (both government-wide financials and fund flow financials), and required supplementary information (RSI). The statistical section includes financial trends, revenue and debt capacity, economic and demographic information, and other data.

Government-Wide Financial Statements and Statement of Net Assets

Government-wide financial statements include a statement of net assets and a statement of activities. The reports are prepared using accrual-based accounting and economic resources measurement. With the exception of fiduciary activities and discriminately reported component units, all activities of the primary government should be documented.

A statement of net assets is a form of balance sheet that uses the equation "assets – liabilities = net assets." Depreciation of fixed assets, including infrastructure, must be calculated and documented, and the statement must follow full accrual accounting methods. "Net assets" have three categories: (a) invested in capital assets, net of related debt, (b) restricted, and (c) unrestricted. The value of capital or fixed assets reduced by accumulated depreciation, further reduced by debt associated with the gaining of the capital assets, determines the value invested in capital assets, net of related debt. Per GASB, restricted means "(a) externally imposed by creditors (such as through debt covenants), grantors, contributors, or laws or regulations of other governments, and (b) imposed by law through constitutional provisions or enabling legislation." In comparison, unrestricted net assets are total assets less invested in capital assets, less related debt and restricted net assets.

Statement of Activities for Government-Wide Financial Statements

A statement of activities for government-wide financial statements documents revenues and expenses utilizing the full accrual method of accounting. When accounting for activities of agreements between governmental and business or between government and discriminately presented component units, the activities are included on the consolidated statement even though they are interfund transactions. The reporting of expenses is by function and the reporting of revenues is by the accrual method. The revenues may be exchange or nonexchange. The exchange revenues are handled in the same manner as for a business. The revenues are recorded at the time the goods or services are transferred for payment. In the case of nonexchange revenue, the government receives something of value, such as property taxes, and does not give something of equal value in return. GASB 33 divides nonexchange revenues into four classes, and how the revenue is recognized depends upon the classification.

The four categories are:

- Derived tax revenues
- Imposed nonexchange revenues
- Government-mandated nonexchange transactions, and
- Voluntary nonexchange transactions.

Governmental Funds Financial Statements

Governmental funds are utilized for general government activities. There are five types of governmental funds: general funds (the most basic operating funds), special revenue funds (funds from particular revenue sources for particular purposes, like road maintenance), debt service funds (funds for the repayment of debt), capital project funds (funds for the construction, maintenance, and acquisition of capital assets), and permanent funds (funds which cannot be expended, like investment funds). Governmental fund financial statements account for the various movements of these types of funds.

Proprietary Funds Financial Statements

Proprietary funds account for any governmental entity's business-like and self-sustaining functions, the same functions which for-profit entities would need to undertake. The accounting equation for proprietary funds is as follows:

(current assets + fixed assets + other assets) = (current liabilities + long-term debt + net assets)

Any financial statement for proprietary funds must distinguish between internal service funds (which account for goods or services provided between or among government departments or agencies to departments or agencies of the same government) and enterprise funds (which account for goods or services provided to non-governmental entities or persons).

Fiduciary Funds Financial Statements

Fiduciary funds account for a governmental entity's responsibilities pertaining to the oversight of agency funds or trust funds for other persons and organizations, both governmental and non-governmental. Examples of fiduciary funds are pension or retirement trust funds, investment trust funds, private purpose trust funds, and a number of agency trust funds. These are all accounted for on the accrual basis. Fiduciary funds financial statements account for the specific movements of these types of funds.

Notes to Financial Statements for Governmental Accounting

While some notes to governmental financial statements are the same as they would be for a profit-seeking business, this is not the case for all of them. All notes which are essential to the financial statements need to be presented, no matter their length. GASB 38 lists a number of required disclosures for the notes, including (1) descriptions of activities accounted for with major funds, internal service fund types, and fiduciary fund types, (2) the length of time meant by "available" in the context of revenue recognition, (3) actions to prevent significant finance-related legal or contractual violations, (4) a schedule detailing changes in short-term debt and why it was issued, (5) changes in the terms of interest rate for variable-rate debt, and other things. GASB 42 also lists a number of required disclosures for the notes pertaining to capital-asset impairment.

MD&A

Management's discussion and analysis (MD&A) is part of the required supplementary information (RSI) for the general purpose external financial report, and even though it is "supplementary," it is nevertheless disclosed before the financial statements. The MD&A should provide

- a brief discussion concerning the basic financial statements, such as relationships between them and different perspectives on the entity which they might give;
- a collection of condensed financial information to compare the current and prior years;
- an analysis of the entity's overall financial position and results of operation;
- an analysis of the balances and transactions of individual funds;

- an analysis of significant budget changes, including any discrepancies between original budget amounts, final budget amounts, and actual expenditures;
- a description of capital asset and long-term liability activity;
- a discussion of infrastructure (for entities using the modified approach); and
- any other significant known facts, events, or conditions which might have bearing on the government's financial situation.

RSI OTHER THAN MANAGEMENT'S DISCUSS AND ANALYSIS

Required supplementary information (RSI) serves to supplement the financial statements and is therefore located after them. A major part of the RSI is the budgetary comparison schedule (BCS), which presents budgetary information for the general fund and for all major special revenue funds, showing the original budget, the final budget, and all fund inflows, outflows, and balances. The BCS ought to be reconciled to GAAP information, which can be done either in a separate schedule or in the footnotes. In addition to the BCS, also included in the RSI should be various infrastructure schedules (for assets reported with the modified approach).

COMBINING STATEMENTS

Combining statements are financial statements which serve to combine the information from multiple funds through separate supporting schedules. These supporting schedules present data which undergird the fund financial statements. Combining statements will also show some of the less major funds discretely, organizing the data according to the type of fund (such as capital projects or debt service).

DERIVATION OF GOVERNMENT-WIDE FINANCIAL STATEMENTS AND RECONCILIATION REQUIREMENTS

Government-wide financial statements are derived from the more basic fund financial statements, and the conversion from fund information to government-wife information occurs at year-end. This includes a number of worksheet adjustments, the elimination of interfund balances, and many other things, with the result being a statement of net assets and a statement of activities. There are two requirements for reconciliation: (1) the fund balance to the total net assets and (2) the change in fund balance to the change in net assets.

GOVERNMENTAL REPORTING ENTITIES

Per the GASB, a financial reporting entity should be based on accountability to the people. All boards, commissions, and agencies that are under the reporting entity must be included. State governments, general local governments, or local governments with a specific task that are separate legally and financially from other state or local governments are defined as a primary government. Within the primary government are component units. The legally separate organization has financial accountability through elected officials of a primary government. If the component unit's correlation with the primary government is not documented, the primary government's financial statements would not be complete. Government-wide entities typically record component units in a separate column or to the right of information related to the primary government on financial statements. If the component units and the primary government activities are so interrelated, then they are deemed to be blended and may be combined to construct a reporting entity. Per GASB 39, a component unit of a government can be composed of a fundraising or similar organization whose major function is to raise or contain considerable resources for the benefit of the particular unit.

Net Position

Net position is itself a component of an entity's statement of financial position, defined according to the GASB as "the residual of all other elements presented in a statement of financial position." The term was formerly "net assets," but the term was changed in order to make the term more general and less focused on economic resources management.

Fund Balance Accounts

Fund balance accounts are the equivalent of equity accounts in governmental accounting, serving as a balancing account rather than denoting the owners' control or interest. They can be subdivided into unreserved fund balance accounts, which mark the difference between assets, liabilities, and fund reserves; and reserved fund accounts, which have a portion of their funds unavailable or reserved for a particular use in the future.

Capital Assets and Infrastructure Assets

Capital assets in governmental accounting are any assets which are utilized in the organization's operations with a useful life that, at the time of acquisition, extends beyond one reporting period. Government managers are generally obligated to uphold and maintain these capital assets as good stewards. Capital assets ought to be accounted for at cost (or estimated cost) and depreciated unless inexhaustible. Infrastructure assets are a kind of capital assets which are significantly long-lived and stationary in nature. Examples of these infrastructure assets are bridges, roads, tunnels, dams, and sewer systems. Buildings, parking lots, and other capital assets which are incidental to property (or access to property) do not qualify as infrastructure assets.

General Long-Term Liabilities

General long-term liabilities are long-term liabilities which arise from the activity of general governmental funds and not from proprietary or fiduciary funds. They are reported as liabilities in the entity's government-wide statement of net assets under the governmental activities column. Most general long-term liabilities are settled through cash payment from a governmental fund.

Interfund Transactions

Interfund transactions are any transactions in governmental accounting which affect two or more funds. Different types of interfund transactions are as follows:

- quasi-external transactions, which would result in recognized revenue and expenses if the entity were not governmental (and should result in such recognition when they occur among governmental funds);
- reimbursements, where one fund receives funds after having been charged expenditures that were properly to be attributed to a different fund;
- interfund transfers, which are non-reciprocal movements among funds which do not expect future repayment; and
- interfund loans.

Nonexchange Transactions

A nonexchange transaction is a transaction where the items exchanged are not equivalent in value, either where the government gives some benefit without receiving equal benefit, or where the government receives some benefit without giving equal benefit. Examples of nonexchange transactions are as follows:

- derived tax revenues, which are imposed on other exchange transactions (e.g. sales taxes and income taxes);
- imposed nonexchange revenues, which arise from government imposition on nongovernmental persons or entities (e.g. property tax);
- government-mandated nonexchange transactions, which occur when a government entity at one level provides resources to another governmental entity at another level with the requirement that the funds be used for a specific purpose; and
- voluntary nonexchange transactions, such as donations.

Classifications of Expenditures of Government Funds per GASB

The five classifications of expenditures of government funds per GASB are as follows:

- Function or program – Gives information on the purpose of expenditures or the service or area of responsibility. (Education, highway, streets, public safety, general government, or health and welfare)
- Organization or department – Assembled per the government's organizational arrangement or the department's responsibility if constant. (Police and fire departments, parks and recreational departments, or personnel departments)
- Activity – The work an organization does as part of its functions or programs. It has more significance if the completion of each activity is fixed. (Police protection including subactivities like administration, traffic control, police training, and support services are typical activities.)
- Character – The expenditures are categorized by the fiscal period that receives the benefit. (Current expenditures, capital outlays, or debt service.)
- Object – The types of items purchased or services obtained define this category. (Supplies, rent, utilities, or buildings.)

Reports that use the category by function include statement of revenues, expenditures, and changes in fund balances. The object category is typically used with budget reports.

Special and Extraordinary Items

In governmental accounting, special items are events which are within management's control but are (1) anomalously large in size and (2) either unusual in nature or rare in occurrence. Extraordinary items are like special items, but they must be both unusual in nature and rare in occurrence in order to qualify. Special and extraordinary items are not considered to be operating inflows or outflows, so they are separately located on the statement of activities after the calculation of excess revenues.

Encumbrances

Encumbrances are restrictions or obligations placed upon budgetary accounts to show how appropriated funds are already required to be spent. They differ from ordinary accounts payable, which represent obligations to pay other parties. At year-end, encumbrance accounts are liquidated and return to the unappropriated fund balance. The amount of unencumbered appropriations can be calculated according to the equation: (unencumbered appropriations) = appropriations – (outstanding encumbrances + year-to-date expenditures)

Requirements that Government Divisions Must Follow per GASB 34

Standards from GASB 34 must be met by typical government divisions to be in compliance with GAAP for reporting:

1. The management's analysis and evaluations.
2. Across the board government financial statement
    a. Net assets statement
    b. Activities statement
3. Fund financial statements
    a. Government funds
    b. Proprietary funds
    c. Fiduciary funds
4. Recording of thoughts regarding financial statement
5. Besides management's views, other information regarding the governing structure are:
    a. Schedule of funding progress
    b. Schedule of employer contributions
    c. Budgetary comparison schedules
    d. Claims development information if government sponsors a public entity risk pool

Financial Statements Required for Governmental Retirement Plans

When governments have retirement plans for their employees, and specifically when they have *defined-benefit pension plans* (meaning that the plan is fundamentally defined by the *benefits* received post-retirement, rather than the *contributions* made pre-retirement), the government is acting as a fiduciary for the benefit of the employees, and hence certain fiduciary financial statements are required. Specifically, the government must have a *statement of fiduciary net position* and a *statement of changes in fiduciary net position*.

In addition, the governmental entity is required to include the following information in the notes to the fiduciary financial statements:

- types of retirement benefits provided
- classes of plan members
- information on the board of directors
- information on investments (investment policies, and the determination of their fair value)

Statement of Fiduciary Net Position and Statement of Changes in Fiduciary Net Position

"Net position" is essentially the governmental or nonprofit equivalent of owners' equity. It represents the residual interest held by a fiduciary: the remaining asset value after liabilities are subtracted. Consequently, a statement of fiduciary net position will have this structure:

(assets + deferred outflows)

– (liabilities + deferred inflows)

= fiduciary net position

A statement of changes in fiduciary net position will have record the various changes in assets and liabilities across a period, having this structure:

additions (contributions + net investment income)

– deductions (benefit payments + administration expenses)

= net change in fiduciary net position

Deferred Inflows and Deferred Outflows

As the name sounds, deferred inflows refer to any inflow of resources for which a governmental entity ought to delay recognition until a later point in time. Deferred outflows are the opposite. For example, if a local government has levied a property tax on its citizens, it can accrue (debit) the funds to be gained from such a levy, but to note that the funds are unavailable at the time of the levy, the entity should *credit* deferred inflows. At a later point in time, the governmental entity can then recognize the availability of the funds by debiting deferred inflows and crediting revenue. This method of accounting allows for assets not yet received to be budgeted for future uses. Note that, as deferred inflows are credited and deferred outflows are debited when first recorded, deferred inflows are grouped with liabilities (though not subsumed under liabilities) when determining net position. That is, deferred outflows *add* to the net position, whereas deferred inflows *subtract* from it.

Nonprofit Accounting and Reporting

Required Financial Statements

All nongovernmental not-for-profit organizations are required to prepare the following financial statements:

- a statement of financial position
- a statement of activities
- a statement of cash flows

The statement of financial position, which documents assets, liabilities, and net assets, must also include organization-wide summations for assets, liabilities, and net assets. The total entity-wide net assets are required to be further classified into unrestricted, temporarily restricted, and permanently restricted. The statement of activities must document revenues, expenses, gains, losses, and reclassifications of net assets, and report organization-wide summations. Changes in net assets for each class must be reported, but individual revenues, expenses, gains, losses, and reclassification for each class may or may not be reported.

Nonprofit Organizations

Typically, nonprofit organizations provide helpful services and do so without seeking a profit. These types of entities may obtain funding from charging users, foundation or individual donor contributions, income from investments, and government grants. How much they receive is dependent upon the type of organization it is. Private sector organizations are nongovernmental and could be a private college, a health care business run by a religious or other nonprofit organization, voluntary health or welfare organizations, or a performing arts or museum type organization. Public sector organizations are governmental and could be a public college, government hospitals, such as veterans' administration hospitals, or government museums.

Categories and General Financial Reporting Guidelines

The four categories of not-for-profit organizations are:

- Colleges and universities
- Health care organizations
- Voluntary health and welfare organizations
- "Other" not-for-profit organizations, such as churches

General financial reporting guidelines include:

- FASB statements 116 and 117, APB opinions, ARB bulletins and other authoritative pronouncements should be applied to the financial statements.
- Financial statements include a statement of financial position, a statement of activities and a statement of cash flows.
- Depreciation is recorded in accordance with Generally Accepted Accounting Principles (GAAP).

Fund accounting is only appropriate for internal reporting.

Standards and Reporting Fund Information

FASB statements 116 and 117, APB opinions, ARB bulletins and other authoritative pronouncements apply to the financial statements of nongovernmental nonprofit organizations, with the exception of those that operate for the direct benefit of their members, such as a mutual insurance company. Funds generally fit into one of three classes: unrestricted, temporarily restricted, or permanently restricted. Resources must be designated restricted by the donors or grantors to be included in the restricted class. Internally designated resources are unrestricted. Another source of restricted funds is contributed resources. Revenues, expenses, gains, and losses are grouped, classified, and reported as increases or decreases in permanently restricted, temporarily restricted, or unrestricted net assets.

Statement of Financial Position

A statement of financial position for a not-for-profit organization must document total assets, total liabilities, and total net assets. The total net assets must be subdivided into unrestricted, temporarily restricted, and permanently restricted. Typically, liquidity and payment date determine how the assets and liabilities are reported. Assets must be separated by function, whether long-term or short term, and reported accordingly. The organization may choose to format the report with the balances by one year or a comparison of two or more years. Contributions receivable are recorded at the present value of future receipts. With investments in securities, if a fair value can be determined, then that amount is used in documentation.

Statement of Activities

The statement of activities is one of the three required financial statements for nongovernmental, not-for-profit organizations. Increases in unrestricted, temporarily restricted, and permanently restricted net assets may come from contributions, income on long-term investments, and net unrealized and realized gains on long-term investments. Unless restricted by donors, all of these revenue sources are considered unrestricted. Exchange revenues, such as admission charges, membership dues, or fees, increase unrestricted net assets. Realized gains, investments, and net unrealized gains are all reported together per FASB. Expenses and losses, for example an actuarial loss, decrease unrestricted net assets. Eventually net assets become unencumbered from their restrictions as temporarily restricted to unrestricted net assets. This may occur due to satisfaction of program restrictions, satisfaction of receipt of equipment restrictions, expiration of time restrictions, or expiration of term endowments. When this occurs, there are adjustments, i.e., decreases and increases, to be made to temporarily restricted assets and unrestricted net assets. The FASB has two specifications: first, expenses are documented by function in the notes to the financial statement, if not in the statement; and second, fund-raising expenses must be similarly documented.

Contributions and income, fees and exchange revenues, and net unrealized and realized gains:

- Contributions are voluntary, nonreciprocal transfers of assets or money to the organization. Along with other income, such as income on long-term investments, and net unrealized and realized gains on long-term investments, these items increase unrestricted, temporarily restricted, and permanently restricted net assets. Unless restricted by donors, the revenue sources increase unrestricted net assets.
- Fees and exchange revenues increase unrestricted net assets. These revenues may include admissions charges, fees, and membership dues.
- Per the FASB, net unrealized and realized gains cannot be displayed separately. Thus net unrealized gains, realized gains, and investments are all recorded together.

STATEMENT OF CASH FLOWS

The statement of cash flows for not-for-profit organizations is quite similar to the same financial statement which for-profit entities must produce, documenting all the movements in cash and cash equivalents. One difference is that with not-for-profit organizations, financing activities must include the inflow of restricted resources that, according to the donor's designation, are reserved for long-term purposes. Moreover, any interest or dividends which are likewise donor-restricted for such long-term purposes should not be included in the statement's section on operating activities.

CONTRIBUTIONS

Contributions are important to not-for-profit organizations since they are often the primary source of revenue. When they are received, they generally are measured at fair value and then categorized as either restricted or unrestricted support, depending upon any purposes for which the donors have stipulated the contributions to be used. Not-for-profit organizations are required to distinguish among contributions received with permanent restrictions, contributions with temporary restrictions, and contributions without any restrictions. Contributions can also be classified as either revenue (if received within the ordinary functioning of the organization) or gains (if received outside the ordinary functioning of the organization).

Multiyear contributions are reported at the present value of the future collections. It is assumed that the monies collected in the future years would be temporarily restricted revenues and each year's receipt reallocated. Contribution revenue ends up being the difference between the amount documented as temporarily restricted revenue at present value and the current value. At the date of the contribution, it should always be reported at fair market value. Donors record the amount given following the same rules as those receiving the contribution.

Contributions and exchange revenues are not the same thing and should not be treated as such. A transaction is considered a contribution if nothing is given by the not-for-profit organization in the exchange. If, however, there are increases in unrestricted net assets caused by tuition, membership dues, or charges for services, then there is an exchange of revenues.

ACCOUNTING METHOD AND REPORTING OF UNCONDITIONAL CONTRIBUTIONS

The full accrual method must be used when reporting revenues, expenses, gains, and losses. Revenue is deemed to be unrestricted unless specifically stated by the donor that it is restricted, either temporarily or permanently. Gross amounts should be used in reporting the revenues and expenses. Gains and losses should be reported using net amounts, as should investment gains and losses.

Unconditional contributions should be reported as assets, contributions receivable, and as revenues, contribution revenue. However, if the donor contributes with restrictions or particular conditions, then the amount is not recognized as a receivable or revenue. The restriction or condition may specify a future or uncertain event whose occurrence or failure to occur may cause the assets to be returned to the contributor or may cause the contribution to be dissolved as if it never occurred.

Permanently Restricted Resources, Temporarily Restricted Resources and Unrestricted Resources

There are three main categories for permanently restricted net assets:

- Specific assets, like artwork that should be specially maintained and shown.
- Endowments that must be invested permanently, with income for either restricted or unrestricted specifications.
- Land that must be held in perpetuity.

With temporarily restricted net assets, there could be an unexpended resource with a specific usage in the future or to be invested for a specific amount of time such as a term endowment. All other resources, such as those from unrestricted contributions, the net amount from providing services, and unrestricted income from investments, can be unrestricted net assets. All resources are considered unrestricted unless specified otherwise.

Net Assets

Net assets in a not-for-profit organization are the residual items left, but are not truly an ownership interest; they are therefore analogous to equity in a for-profit entity. Different types of net assets are unrestricted net assets, temporarily restricted net assets, and permanently restricted net assets. All of these categorizations involve restrictions detailed by the donors on their own contributions. Net assets are sometimes reclassified from temporarily restricted to unrestricted for the satisfaction of program restrictions, acquiring equipment restrictions, expiration of time restrictions, or expiration of term endowments. This causes increases in unrestricted net assets and decreases in temporarily restricted net assets.

Long-Lived Assets

Long-lived assets are any assets held by not-for-profit organizations intended to remain in use for the long term, such as property and equipment (or assets for the acquisition of property and equipment). All donations of long-lived assets which are received with no donor-imposed stipulations concerning the length of use for the asset should be reported as restricted support, so long as the entity's accounting policy implies a time restriction which expires over the course of the asset's useful life. Without such a policy, however, the lack of any donors' stipulations leads to the classification of such assets as unrestricted long-lived assets. The donation of unrestricted long-lived assets ought to be reported as operating revenue if the donation occurs as part of the entity's ordinary operations, and as nonoperating gains if it does not. The donation of restricted long-lived assets ought to be reported as restricted gains or revenue.

Expenses

Expenses for not-for-profit organizations need to tracked and categorized according to the nature of the expense and the function of the expense. Natural expense categories include such items as salaries, rent, professional fees, and office supplies, while functional expense categories include such items as program expenses and general and administrative expenses. (Program expenses should be divided according to specific programs and accounted for separately.) Nonprofit entities also ought to disclose depreciation expenses for the term, depreciable asset balances (according to the asset's nature of function_, accumulated depreciation (whether in total or according to major classes of assets), and the depreciation method utilized. Depreciation does not apply to artwork or to other pieces of antiquity.

Investments

A key way for nonprofit organizations to make use of their revenue and increase their total funds for use it with sound investments. Whatever income a not-for-profit entity earns with investments, such as interest or dividends, should be reported in the organization's statement of activities as adjustments to unrestricted net assets (unless a restriction exists), and all applicable investments ought to be recognized according to their fair value, with the appropriate gains and losses also recorded.

Disclosures Made on Investments

A not-for-profit organization ought to disclose a number of details concerning its investments, including the composition of its return on investment, a reconciliation of its return on investment to whatever is recorded in the statement of activities, the carrying amount (and the basis for the carrying amount) of the different major types of investments, the methods used to discern the fair value of securities, the total amount of deficiencies related to donor-restricted endowment funds according to which the assets' fair value at the reporting date is less than what the donors stipulated, and the nature and book value for each group of investments which constitutes a concentration of risk.

How to Overcome Test Anxiety

Just the thought of taking a test is enough to make most people a little nervous. A test is an important event that can have a long-term impact on your future, so it's important to take it seriously and it's natural to feel anxious about performing well. But just because anxiety is normal, that doesn't mean that it's helpful in test taking, or that you should simply accept it as part of your life. Anxiety can have a variety of effects. These effects can be mild, like making you feel slightly nervous, or severe, like blocking your ability to focus or remember even a simple detail.

If you experience test anxiety—whether severe or mild—it's important to know how to beat it. To discover this, first you need to understand what causes test anxiety.

Causes of Test Anxiety

While we often think of anxiety as an uncontrollable emotional state, it can actually be caused by simple, practical things. One of the most common causes of test anxiety is that a person does not feel adequately prepared for their test. This feeling can be the result of many different issues such as poor study habits or lack of organization, but the most common culprit is time management. Starting to study too late, failing to organize your study time to cover all of the material, or being distracted while you study will mean that you're not well prepared for the test. This may lead to cramming the night before, which will cause you to be physically and mentally exhausted for the test. Poor time management also contributes to feelings of stress, fear, and hopelessness as you realize you are not well prepared but don't know what to do about it.

Other times, test anxiety is not related to your preparation for the test but comes from unresolved fear. This may be a past failure on a test, or poor performance on tests in general. It may come from comparing yourself to others who seem to be performing better or from the stress of living up to expectations. Anxiety may be driven by fears of the future—how failure on this test would affect your educational and career goals. These fears are often completely irrational, but they can still negatively impact your test performance.

Elements of Test Anxiety

As mentioned earlier, test anxiety is considered to be an emotional state, but it has physical and mental components as well. Sometimes you may not even realize that you are suffering from test anxiety until you notice the physical symptoms. These can include trembling hands, rapid heartbeat, sweating, nausea, and tense muscles. Extreme anxiety may lead to fainting or vomiting. Obviously, any of these symptoms can have a negative impact on testing. It is important to recognize them as soon as they begin to occur so that you can address the problem before it damages your performance.

The mental components of test anxiety include trouble focusing and inability to remember learned information. During a test, your mind is on high alert, which can help you recall information and stay focused for an extended period of time. However, anxiety interferes with your mind's natural processes, causing you to blank out, even on the questions you know well. The strain of testing during anxiety makes it difficult to stay focused, especially on a test that may take several hours. Extreme anxiety can take a huge mental toll, making it difficult not only to recall test information but even to understand the test questions or pull your thoughts together.

Effects of Test Anxiety

Test anxiety is like a disease—if left untreated, it will get progressively worse. Anxiety leads to poor performance, and this reinforces the feelings of fear and failure, which in turn lead to poor performances on subsequent tests. It can grow from a mild nervousness to a crippling condition. If allowed to progress, test anxiety can have a big impact on your schooling, and consequently on your future.

Test anxiety can spread to other parts of your life. Anxiety on tests can become anxiety in any stressful situation, and blanking on a test can turn into panicking in a job situation. But fortunately, you don't have to let anxiety rule your testing and determine your grades. There are a number of relatively simple steps you can take to move past anxiety and function normally on a test and in the rest of life.

Physical Steps for Beating Test Anxiety

While test anxiety is a serious problem, the good news is that it can be overcome. It doesn't have to control your ability to think and remember information. While it may take time, you can begin taking steps today to beat anxiety.

Just as your first hint that you may be struggling with anxiety comes from the physical symptoms, the first step to treating it is also physical. Rest is crucial for having a clear, strong mind. If you are tired, it is much easier to give in to anxiety. But if you establish good sleep habits, your body and mind will be ready to perform optimally, without the strain of exhaustion. Additionally, sleeping well helps you to retain information better, so you're more likely to recall the answers when you see the test questions.

Getting good sleep means more than going to bed on time. It's important to allow your brain time to relax. Take study breaks from time to time so it doesn't get overworked, and don't study right before bed. Take time to rest your mind before trying to rest your body, or you may find it difficult to fall asleep.

Along with sleep, other aspects of physical health are important in preparing for a test. Good nutrition is vital for good brain function. Sugary foods and drinks may give a burst of energy but this burst is followed by a crash, both physically and emotionally. Instead, fuel your body with protein and vitamin-rich foods.

Also, drink plenty of water. Dehydration can lead to headaches and exhaustion, especially if your brain is already under stress from the rigors of the test. Particularly if your test is a long one, drink water during the breaks. And if possible, take an energy-boosting snack to eat between sections.

Along with sleep and diet, a third important part of physical health is exercise. Maintaining a steady workout schedule is helpful, but even taking 5-minute study breaks to walk can help get your blood pumping faster and clear your head. Exercise also releases endorphins, which contribute to a positive feeling and can help combat test anxiety.

When you nurture your physical health, you are also contributing to your mental health. If your body is healthy, your mind is much more likely to be healthy as well. So take time to rest, nourish your body with healthy food and water, and get moving as much as possible. Taking these physical steps will make you stronger and more able to take the mental steps necessary to overcome test anxiety.

Mental Steps for Beating Test Anxiety

Working on the mental side of test anxiety can be more challenging, but as with the physical side, there are clear steps you can take to overcome it. As mentioned earlier, test anxiety often stems from lack of preparation, so the obvious solution is to prepare for the test. Effective studying may be the most important weapon you have for beating test anxiety, but you can and should employ several other mental tools to combat fear.

First, boost your confidence by reminding yourself of past success—tests or projects that you aced. If you're putting as much effort into preparing for this test as you did for those, there's no reason you should expect to fail here. Work hard to prepare; then trust your preparation.

Second, surround yourself with encouraging people. It can be helpful to find a study group, but be sure that the people you're around will encourage a positive attitude. If you spend time with others who are anxious or cynical, this will only contribute to your own anxiety. Look for others who are motivated to study hard from a desire to succeed, not from a fear of failure.

Third, reward yourself. A test is physically and mentally tiring, even without anxiety, and it can be helpful to have something to look forward to. Plan an activity following the test, regardless of the outcome, such as going to a movie or getting ice cream.

When you are taking the test, if you find yourself beginning to feel anxious, remind yourself that you know the material. Visualize successfully completing the test. Then take a few deep, relaxing breaths and return to it. Work through the questions carefully but with confidence, knowing that you are capable of succeeding.

Developing a healthy mental approach to test taking will also aid in other areas of life. Test anxiety affects more than just the actual test—it can be damaging to your mental health and even contribute to depression. It's important to beat test anxiety before it becomes a problem for more than testing.

Study Strategy

Being prepared for the test is necessary to combat anxiety, but what does being prepared look like? You may study for hours on end and still not feel prepared. What you need is a strategy for test prep. The next few pages outline our recommended steps to help you plan out and conquer the challenge of preparation.

Step 1: Scope Out the Test

Learn everything you can about the format (multiple choice, essay, etc.) and what will be on the test. Gather any study materials, course outlines, or sample exams that may be available. Not only will this help you to prepare, but knowing what to expect can help to alleviate test anxiety.

Step 2: Map Out the Material

Look through the textbook or study guide and make note of how many chapters or sections it has. Then divide these over the time you have. For example, if a book has 15 chapters and you have five days to study, you need to cover three chapters each day. Even better, if you have the time, leave an extra day at the end for overall review after you have gone through the material in depth.

If time is limited, you may need to prioritize the material. Look through it and make note of which sections you think you already have a good grasp on, and which need review. While you are studying, skim quickly through the familiar sections and take more time on the challenging parts.

Write out your plan so you don't get lost as you go. Having a written plan also helps you feel more in control of the study, so anxiety is less likely to arise from feeling overwhelmed at the amount to cover.

Step 3: Gather Your Tools

Decide what study method works best for you. Do you prefer to highlight in the book as you study and then go back over the highlighted portions? Or do you type out notes of the important information? Or is it helpful to make flashcards that you can carry with you? Assemble the pens, index cards, highlighters, post-it notes, and any other materials you may need so you won't be distracted by getting up to find things while you study.

If you're having a hard time retaining the information or organizing your notes, experiment with different methods. For example, try color-coding by subject with colored pens, highlighters, or post-it notes. If you learn better by hearing, try recording yourself reading your notes so you can listen while in the car, working out, or simply sitting at your desk. Ask a friend to quiz you from your flashcards, or try teaching someone the material to solidify it in your mind.

Step 4: Create Your Environment

It's important to avoid distractions while you study. This includes both the obvious distractions like visitors and the subtle distractions like an uncomfortable chair (or a too-comfortable couch that makes you want to fall asleep). Set up the best study environment possible: good lighting and a comfortable work area. If background music helps you focus, you may want to turn it on, but otherwise keep the room quiet. If you are using a computer to take notes, be sure you don't have any other windows open, especially applications like social media, games, or anything else that could distract you. Silence your phone and turn off notifications. Be sure to keep water close by so you stay hydrated while you study (but avoid unhealthy drinks and snacks).

Also, take into account the best time of day to study. Are you freshest first thing in the morning? Try to set aside some time then to work through the material. Is your mind clearer in the afternoon or evening? Schedule your study session then. Another method is to study at the same time of day that you will take the test, so that your brain gets used to working on the material at that time and will be ready to focus at test time.

Step 5: Study!

Once you have done all the study preparation, it's time to settle into the actual studying. Sit down, take a few moments to settle your mind so you can focus, and begin to follow your study plan. Don't give in to distractions or let yourself procrastinate. This is your time to prepare so you'll be ready to fearlessly approach the test. Make the most of the time and stay focused.

Of course, you don't want to burn out. If you study too long you may find that you're not retaining the information very well. Take regular study breaks. For example, taking five minutes out of every hour to walk briskly, breathing deeply and swinging your arms, can help your mind stay fresh.

As you get to the end of each chapter or section, it's a good idea to do a quick review. Remind yourself of what you learned and work on any difficult parts. When you feel that you've mastered the material, move on to the next part. At the end of your study session, briefly skim through your notes again.

But while review is helpful, cramming last minute is NOT. If at all possible, work ahead so that you won't need to fit all your study into the last day. Cramming overloads your brain with more information than it can process and retain, and your tired mind may struggle to recall even previously learned information when it is overwhelmed with last-minute study. Also, the urgent nature of cramming and the stress placed on your brain contribute to anxiety. You'll be more likely to go to the test feeling unprepared and having trouble thinking clearly.

So don't cram, and don't stay up late before the test, even just to review your notes at a leisurely pace. Your brain needs rest more than it needs to go over the information again. In fact, plan to finish your studies by noon or early afternoon the day before the test. Give your brain the rest of the day to relax or focus on other things, and get a good night's sleep. Then you will be fresh for the test and better able to recall what you've studied.

Step 6: Take a Practice Test

Many courses offer sample tests, either online or in the study materials. This is an excellent resource to check whether you have mastered the material, as well as to prepare for the test format and environment.

Check the test format ahead of time: the number of questions, the type (multiple choice, free response, etc.), and the time limit. Then create a plan for working through them. For example, if you have 30 minutes to take a 60-question test, your limit is 30 seconds per question. Spend less time on the questions you know well so that you can take more time on the difficult ones.

If you have time to take several practice tests, take the first one open book, with no time limit. Work through the questions at your own pace and make sure you fully understand them. Gradually work up to taking a test under test conditions: sit at a desk with all study materials put away and set a timer. Pace yourself to make sure you finish the test with time to spare and go back to check your answers if you have time.

After each test, check your answers. On the questions you missed, be sure you understand why you missed them. Did you misread the question (tests can use tricky wording)? Did you forget the information? Or was it something you hadn't learned? Go back and study any shaky areas that the practice tests reveal.

Taking these tests not only helps with your grade, but also aids in combating test anxiety. If you're already used to the test conditions, you're less likely to worry about it, and working through tests until you're scoring well gives you a confidence boost. Go through the practice tests until you feel comfortable, and then you can go into the test knowing that you're ready for it.

Test Tips

On test day, you should be confident, knowing that you've prepared well and are ready to answer the questions. But aside from preparation, there are several test day strategies you can employ to maximize your performance.

First, as stated before, get a good night's sleep the night before the test (and for several nights before that, if possible). Go into the test with a fresh, alert mind rather than staying up late to study.

Try not to change too much about your normal routine on the day of the test. It's important to eat a nutritious breakfast, but if you normally don't eat breakfast at all, consider eating just a protein bar. If you're a coffee drinker, go ahead and have your normal coffee. Just make sure you time it so that the caffeine doesn't wear off right in the middle of your test. Avoid sugary beverages, and drink enough water to stay hydrated but not so much that you need a restroom break 10 minutes into the test. If your test isn't first thing in the morning, consider going for a walk or doing a light workout before the test to get your blood flowing.

Allow yourself enough time to get ready, and leave for the test with plenty of time to spare so you won't have the anxiety of scrambling to arrive in time. Another reason to be early is to select a good seat. It's helpful to sit away from doors and windows, which can be distracting. Find a good seat, get out your supplies, and settle your mind before the test begins.

When the test begins, start by going over the instructions carefully, even if you already know what to expect. Make sure you avoid any careless mistakes by following the directions.

Then begin working through the questions, pacing yourself as you've practiced. If you're not sure on an answer, don't spend too much time on it, and don't let it shake your confidence. Either skip it and come back later, or eliminate as many wrong answers as possible and guess among the remaining ones. Don't dwell on these questions as you continue—put them out of your mind and focus on what lies ahead.

Be sure to read all of the answer choices, even if you're sure the first one is the right answer. Sometimes you'll find a better one if you keep reading. But don't second-guess yourself if you do immediately know the answer. Your gut instinct is usually right. Don't let test anxiety rob you of the information you know.

If you have time at the end of the test (and if the test format allows), go back and review your answers. Be cautious about changing any, since your first instinct tends to be correct, but make sure you didn't misread any of the questions or accidentally mark the wrong answer choice. Look over any you skipped and make an educated guess.

At the end, leave the test feeling confident. You've done your best, so don't waste time worrying about your performance or wishing you could change anything. Instead, celebrate the successful completion of this test. And finally, use this test to learn how to deal with anxiety even better next time.

Review Video: Test Anxiety
Visit mometrix.com/academy and enter code: 100340

Important Qualification

Not all anxiety is created equal. If your test anxiety is causing major issues in your life beyond the classroom or testing center, or if you are experiencing troubling physical symptoms related to your anxiety, it may be a sign of a serious physiological or psychological condition. If this sounds like your situation, we strongly encourage you to seek professional help.

Online Resources

Due to our efforts to try to keep this book to a manageable length, we've created a link that will give you access to all of your online resources:

mometrix.com/resources719/cpafinacctrep

It's Your Moment, Let's Celebrate It!

Share your story @mometrixtestpreparation